Exploring Math & Science in Preschool

From the editors of *Teaching Young Children*

Exploring
Math & Science
in Preschool

From the editors of *Teaching Young Children*

National Association for the Education of Young Children
Washington, DC

National Association for the Education
of Young Children

NAEYC Publishing

Chief Publishing Officer
Derry Koralek

Editor-in-Chief
Kathy Charner

Director of Creative Services
Edwin C. Malstrom

Managing Editor
Mary Jaffe

Senior Editor
Holly Bohart

Senior Graphic Designer
Malini Dominey

Designer
Victoria Moy

Associate Editor
Meghan Dombrink-Green

Associate Editor
Elizabeth Wegner

Assistant Editor
Lauren Baker

Editorial Assistant
Ryan Smith

Through its publications program, the National Association for the Education of Young Children (NAEYC) provides a forum for discussion of major issues and ideas in the early childhood field, with the hope of provoking thought and promoting professional growth. The views expressed or implied in this book are not necessarily those of the Association or its members.

Permissions

"Ready, Set, Learn! We're Off to the Moon" is adapted from activities in *Thinking BIG, Learning BIG: Connecting Science, Math, Literacy, and Language in Early Childhood,* by Marie Faust Evitt (Gryphon House, 2009).

Credits

Photographs: Copyright © Steve Baccom/Digital Vision/Thinkstock: 80; Bonnie Blagojevic: 7; Vadym Boyshenko/iStock/Thinkstock: 32; Bill Brinson: 52 (right), 55 (top); carroteater/iStock/Thinkstock: vi (top right), 38 (right); Sandra Lighter-Jones: 13; Jeffery Koh/iStock/Thinkstock: 33; Lois Main: 28 (right); NAEYC: 4 (left), 35, 39, 40 (left), 41 (left), 100 (top left), 101 (top); Elisabeth Nichols: v (bottom), 5, 6, 8, 100 (bottom); Marilyn Nolt: 24; Karen Phillips: vi (bottom right), vii (top), 4 (right), 26, 27 (top and bottom), 28 (left), 29 (top and bottom), 42, 43 (bottom), 52 (left), 53, 54 (left and right), 55 (bottom), 99, 101 (top), 102; Shari Schmidt: v (top); Ellen Senisi: vi (left), 10, 14 (left and right), 25, 98, 101 (bottom); University of Maine CCIDS: 56 (left and right); Maria Wynne: 38 (left), 40 (right), 41 (right), 43 (top), 100 (top right)
Courtesy of article authors: vii (middle and bottom), 34, 36, 37, 44–49, 58–63, 72–75, 79, 81–83, 88–93
Courtesy of the Freeburg Early Childhood Program in Waterloo, Iowa: 84–87
Illustrations: Copyright © Jennifer O'Connell

Exploring Math and Science in Preschool.

Copyright © 2015 by the National Association for the Education of Young Children. All rights reserved. Printed in the United States of America.

Library of Congress Control Number: 2014945389
ISBN: 978-1-938113-09-3
Item 7226

CONTENTS

1 INTRODUCTION
by Meghan Dombrink-Green

MATH

4 Discovering Shapes and Space in Preschool
by Linda Dauksas and Jeanne White

10 Discovering Math and Science Concepts Through Unit Blocks
by Karyn W. Tunks

16 Math and Manipulatives Learning Center
by Laura J. Colker

20 A Place for Making Games and Puzzles
by Laura J. Colker

24 You Can Count on Math
by Laura J. Colker

30 Books About Counting to 10 and Higher
by Lauren Baker

32 Using Children's Books to Introduce Math
by Sarah Normandie

35 Preschoolers Getting in Shape
by Julie Sarama and Douglas H. Clements

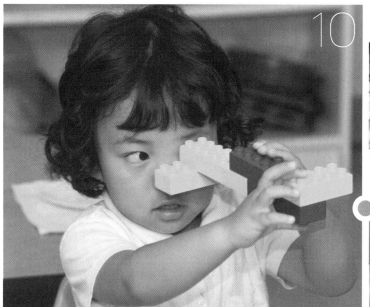

38 **Everyday Math Manipulatives**
by Meghan Dombrink-Green

40 **Sorting Activities for Preschoolers**
by William C. Ritz

44 **Developing Math Games Based on Children's Books**
by Kay M. Cutler, Deanna Gilkerson, Sue Parrott, and Mary Teresa Bowne

50 **Math and Manipulatives Learning Center Checklist**
by Laura J. Colker

SCIENCE

52 **Exploring Motion**
by Elizabeth A. Sherwood and Amy Freshwater

58 **Creatures in Your Gardening Curriculum**
by Alyse C. Hachey and Deanna Butler

64 **Discovering Science Learning Center**
by Laura J. Colker

68 **A Place for Studying Our Bodies**
by Laura J. Colker

72 **Exploring Trees**
by Ellen Hall, Desarie Kennedy, Alison Maher, and
Lisa Stevens

76 **Books About Underwater Life**
by Lauren Baker

78 **Worms to Beans**
by Jean Thompson Bird

81 **Let's Find Out! Preschoolers as Scientific Explorers**
by Kimberly Brenneman

84 **Ramps and Pathways: Physical Science for Preschoolers**
by Betty Zan and Rosemary Geiken

88 **Ready, Set, Learn! We're Off to the Moon**
by Marie Faust Evitt

94 **Discovering Science Learning Center Checklist**
by Laura J. Colker

96 **CREDITS**

98 **ABOUT THE AUTHORS**

Introduction

Meghan Dombrink-Green

A few years ago my nephew Sean, then 3 years old, developed an interest in birds. He started a collection after he saw plush birds in a museum gift shop. The perfect size for preschoolers' hands, the birds make authentic bird calls when squeezed. Sean likes to play, arrange, and cuddle with them. He settles the birds in their nest—which sometimes lives next to his bed—and he often falls asleep with one or two of them. He has a scarlet tanager, an oriole, and a turkey, among others. For birthdays and holidays, family members have given him these plush birds and taken great delight in seeing his interest in birds grow.

During the first year of this phase Sean wanted to dress up for Halloween as one of his favorite birds—a red-winged blackbird. He wore black sweatpants, a black sweatshirt with yellow and red tape on his upper arms, and black wings that his father fashioned from a broken umbrella. The next Halloween Sean wanted to be a painted bunting, a colorful bird from the cardinal family. Having heard "What are you?" a lot the year

before, Sean and his parents brought the plush bird with them the second year. As they trick-or-treated, they met a neighbor who recognized Sean's costume because he had lived in Oklahoma, one of the states where painted buntings live.

I love this story because it not only talks about why my nephew dressed up like a bird for two Halloweens, but it also reflects Sean's science and math explorations. From the beginning the plush birds taught Sean about similarities and differences. All birds have wings, but different types of birds make different sounds. He learned about habitats and building a nest. When he met the neighbor who recognized his costume, Sean learned about migration patterns. His parents introduced the word *migrate* and explained how and why birds fly to different places. Sean explored math concepts and numbers when he realized he had too many birds to fit in one nest. He had to count to see how many fit and how many didn't.

Sean's passion for birds has taught him a lot about

science and math. And just as Sean's sustained interest has helped him explore these concepts, similar projects and activities can help preschoolers learn.

About This Book

From materials to activities, puzzles to worms, the content in this book offers practical strategies and engaging visuals to help teachers support preschoolers' explorations of math and science. Ideas are organized into two sections: math and science. Each section features ideas and activities related to that topic, as well as useful tips so teachers can immediately try these strategies in the classroom. At the end of each section is a checklist to help you review how you and the children use math and science-related learning centers.

Through bright drawings, the learning center illustrations showcase innovative ways to design, arrange, and implement best practices. The accompanying text identifies what children do and learn in a particular center, how the center can include children's families and cultures, tips for setting up the center, and suggestions for stretching your budget.

The tips for supporting dual language learners describe ways to help children who are learning two or more languages at the same time. These tips were written by Karen N. Nemeth, author of *Basics of Supporting Dual Language Learners* (NAEYC, 2012).

The Reflective Questions help you think about yourself as a teacher and about the specific children in your program. The Reflective Questions Thinking Lens®, which is a way of examining your teaching practice, comes from Deb Curtis and colleagues at Harvest Resources Associates, LLC.

The ideas in this book support the development and learning of all preschoolers. For example, while some children may prefer to play alone or spend all their time in one center, almost all children love to explore nature. And while digging in the dirt may look like a mess, educators know that from this thoroughly enjoyable activity children can learn about insects, natural materials, and the environment—all key scientific topics. Teachers can use the suggestions in this book to individualize activities and scaffold children's learning.

Before you finish reading this book, think about the children in your program. Who is especially good at creating patterns? Who loves to stomp in mud puddles? Who could spend hours watching ants? Children are already fascinated by math and science. They just use different terms. Use the suggestions and activities in this book to extend children's knowledge and understanding of favorite topics. It's likely that there are wonderful math or science opportunities within them.

Sean's most recent bird is a dark-eyed junco, and I will ask him about it the next time I see him. He'll probably be able to tell me about the bird's colors, what it sounds like, and where it lives. He won't do this because he had a science lesson about birds, but because he loves birds and wants to learn all about them. We hope this book will inspire you and the children you work with to find the innate math and science in the things you love to learn about.

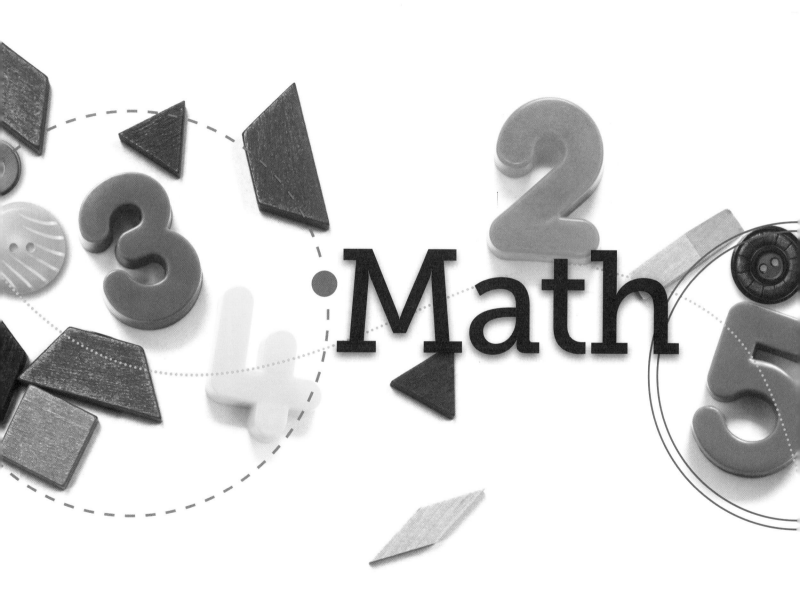

Discovering Shapes and Space in Preschool

Linda Dauksas and Jeanne White

P reschool teachers can create environments in which children are eager to explore and learn about math. They can provide developmentally appropriate materials and opportunities to help preschoolers understand the topic. Math can be a part of daily routines, activities, and interactions in preschool.

The Common Core State Standards for Mathematics (CCSSM) are written to ensure students will leave school ready for work and college. In the CCSSM, two critical areas make up kindergarten content. The first is representing, relating, and operating on whole numbers with sets of objects. The second is describing shapes and space (National Governors Association Center for Best Practices & Council of Chief State School Officers 2010). By the end of kindergarten, children need to demonstrate understanding by analyzing, comparing, creating, and composing these shapes. Preschool teachers have numerous opportunities to help children begin to develop their understanding of shapes and space.

Recognize and Compare Two- and Three-Dimensional Shapes

In preschool, children can learn to identify and name *circles*, *triangles*, *squares*, *rectangles*, and *ovals*. By using materials such as posters, blocks, books, and games, teachers expose children to various shapes and help them analyze *two-* and *three-dimensional shapes* in various sizes and orientations.

The following strategies and activities can help preschoolers learn to recognize and compare shapes.

- **Identify shapes.** Introduce children to different kinds of triangles, such as *equilateral, isosceles, scalene,* and *right.* After finding them in the classroom or outdoors, children can outline the triangles with colored tape. For example, they might make right triangles red and scalene triangles blue.
- **Introduce math words.** Create a math word wall or incorporate mathematical words into the existing word wall—color-code the math words to make it easier for children to notice them. Be sure to write math words in English and in children's home languages. Teachers can use real objects, photos, and black line drawings to define the words.
- **Compare shapes.** Ask children to identify different sizes of the same shape. For example, in the classroom they could search for rectangles, such as windows, doors, books, shelves, cabinets, computer screens, tabletops, and cubbies. Next, help children think as they compare the sizes of rectangles. "The door is bigger than the cubbies."

"The cubbies are bigger than the book, but they are all rectangles." Encourage children to do the same with triangles, circles, and other shapes.

- **What's the difference?** Explain the differences between *two-dimensional* (flat) shapes and *three-dimensional* (solid) shapes. "How are the book and piece of construction paper the same?" "How are they different?"
- **Create a shape-scape.** Teachers and families can collect three-dimensional objects such as cans, cartons, boxes, and balls to create a shape-scape. Children can use *cylinders* (paper towel rolls) as tree trunks, *spheres* (balls) as treetops, and *rectangular prisms* (cereal boxes) as buildings. Teachers and children can work together to label the shape-scape, count the number of shapes used, and plan additions to the structure.

- **Go from 3-D to 2-D.** Preschoolers can dip three-dimensional objects in paints and press them on paper to make prints. Cans, spools, candles, and drinking glasses work well. The children will see the flat shapes that make up the sides of the objects.
- **Discover shapes outdoors.** Look for manhole covers, flags, windows, signs, and other distinct shapes. Working together, children and teachers can take photos of the shapes, label them in the photos, and assemble the photos into a class book.
- **Learn new vocabulary.** Introduce words such as *thick, thin, small, large, long, short, facet, slide, flip,* and *turn* in English and home languages during meal and snack times. Offer snacks with various dimensions and encourage children to use comparative words when asking for food. "I'd like the long carrot, please." Add these descriptive words to the word wall.

- **Play shape Hokey Pokey.** Have each preschooler hold a shape and put it in the circle instead of a body part. "Put your square in. Take your square out. Do the Hokey Pokey and turn yourself around."
- **Play a shape guessing game.** Have preschoolers play in pairs. Explain that one child will hide the shape behind her back and the other will ask questions about the shape. "Does the shape have three sides?" "Does the shape have four angles?"
- **Offer geoband challenges.** Teachers can offer geoboards and geobands so children can create as many different shapes as possible. Provide an additional challenge by asking children to color-code the shapes.

Create and Take Apart Shapes

Once preschoolers can correctly identify flat (*square, circle, triangle, rectangle, hexagon*) and solid or three-dimensional shapes (*cube, cone, cylinder, rectangular prism, sphere*), they are ready to create and then take apart shapes using materials provided by their teacher.

- **Make a shape.** Offer toothpicks, pipe cleaners, straws, or craft sticks as materials children can use to make into shapes. Discuss the shapes they make. "That's a triangle." "How could you turn it into a square?"
- **Create new shapes.** Children can glue together two or more shapes cut from paper onto a blank piece of paper to form other shapes. "You glued two triangles together to form a rectangle."

- **Create solid shapes.** Children can roll, pinch, and manipulate playdough or clay to make two or more shapes. Then they can combine their creations to make new shapes.
- **Deconstruct shapes.** Children can explore how to form three-dimensional shapes. For example, let children watch as you cut rectangular prism shaped containers such as cereal boxes. "How many rectangular pieces did I cut from the box?" Then ask children to figure out how to put them back together.
- **Play with tangrams.** Have several sets of tangrams and pattern cards on hand. Children can start by laying tans on each pattern. They can progress to re-creating the pattern on another surface and making up their own patterns.
- **Build a hexagon puzzle.** Cut one hexagon into trapezoids and triangles. Invite children to use those pieces to fill in another hexagon of the same size.

Spatial Visualization

Encourage preschoolers to slide, flip, or turn shapes to promote problem solving and an understanding of transformations. These transformations are crucial to developing spatial visualization abilities and understanding geometry, which involves matching shapes through visualization.

- **Use the correct terms.** A turn is a *rotation*. A flip is a *reflection*. A slide is a *translation*.
- **Send pattern cards and tangrams home.** Encourage families to play, discover, and name transformations at home as they duplicate figures on the cards. "Can you rotate the triangle to fit the figure?" "I saw you slide the rectangle."
- **Play a transformation game.** Give children dolls or stuffed toys and point out the front and back of each toy. Call out directions—"flip your doll up, turn your teddy bear on its side"—to see if preschoolers can demonstrate the transformations. After they master flipping the toys, have the children practice with shape pieces.
- **Play Mirror, Mirror.** Give each child a single set of pattern blocks and a small mirror. Ask children to create a design with their blocks. Then have them hold the mirror up to each side of the design to see how it appears to be flipped in the mirror.

Spatial Orientation

As preschoolers learn to identify objects, they can use spatial orientation vocabulary to describe the relative positions of objects. Preschoolers should understand and be able to use positional words such as *above, below, beside, in front of, behind, next to, between, on, over, under*, and *inside*.

- **Focus on a word a week.** Introduce the word in English and children's home languages. Use the word throughout the day in the classroom, in the hallway, and on the playground. "You are sitting al lado de a friend." "Place your napkin beside the plate." "Stand beside your partner."
- **Pair positional and shape vocabulary.** "The clock is a circle. It is beside the door, which is a rectangle."
- **Create a book.** Invite families to write about a favorite activity using positional words. "We drove next to the park, traveled under the expressway, and walked over the bridge." Children can provide the illustrations.
- **Use photo examples.** Take photos of the children demonstrating positional concepts. "Hong is standing under the clock." Add photos and words to the word wall.
- **Play spatial Simon Says.** Give each child in a small group a stuffed animal and play Simon Says using positional vocabulary. "Simon Says put your animal above your head." "Put your animal under your chair."
- **Create positional obstacle courses.** Encourage preschoolers' use of positional words during play or transitions. "Before going outside, climb up the steps, slide down the slide, jump over the cones, and line up next to the door."
- **Narrate actions with orientation.** Use positional words to describe how the children move from one place to another. "You parked your trikes on the playground and next to the window." "You walked under the skylight and over the carpet to enter the classroom."

Conclusion

Preschool teachers can create environments and plan activities so young children and their families are both enveloped and engaged in mathematics. Programs can feature numeric and geometric representations with appropriate vocabulary terms. Beyond the classroom, preschoolers can discover and enjoy mathematics in their homes and communities.

REFERENCE

National Governors Association Center for Best Practices & Council of Chief State School Officers. 2010. "Mathematics Standards, K–12." Washington, DC: NGA & CCSSO. www.corestandards.org/math.

RESOURCES

Copley, J.V. 2010. *The Young Child and Mathematics.* 2nd ed. Washington, DC: NAEYC; Reston, VA: NCTM.

Shillady, A., ed. 2012. *Spotlight on Young Children: Exploring Math.* Washington, DC: NAEYC.

Zubrzycki, J. 2011. "Common Core Poses Challenges for Preschools." *Education Week* 31 (13): 1, 20–21.

Transformations

These are transformations:

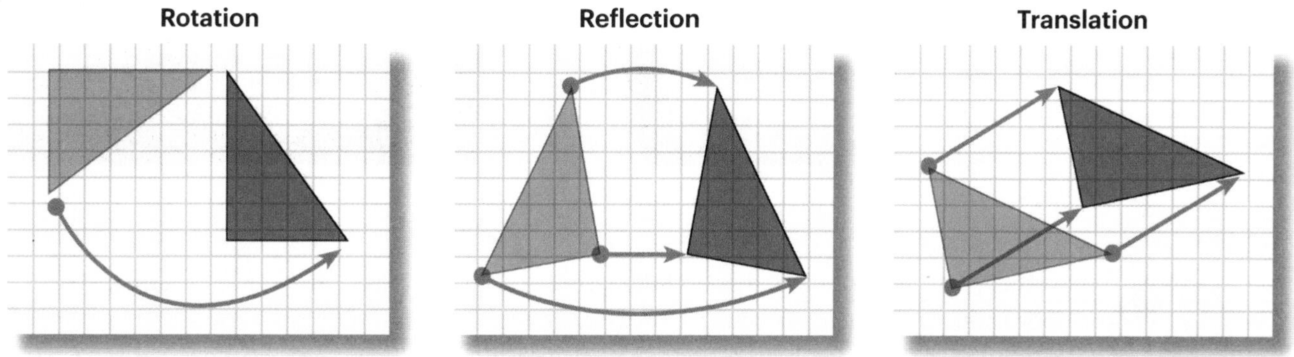

Rotation   **Reflection**   **Translation**

After any of these transformations, the shape still has the same size, area, angles, and line lengths.

Discovering Math and Science Concepts Through Unit Blocks

Karyn W. Tunks

Four-year-olds Frank and Latoya are rebuilding a racetrack and garage they made last week. Having already agreed on the design, they quickly begin placing double unit blocks end to end, adding curved blocks as needed to make an oval racetrack. They use longer blocks to make the garage floor and place ramps side by side on one end for vehicles to enter. To embellish the structure they add pillars on either side of the track and top them with an arched block. After a suggestion from their teacher, they create a tunnel for cars to pass through by repeating the pillar-and-arch structure.

hile other play and learning materials have come and gone, blocks continue to be a mainstay in preschool classrooms. Their smooth wooden surfaces and standard proportions make them inviting to young builders and allow them to pose and solve problems and discover math concepts. The resiliency of the material allows a set of blocks to last for generations.

Planning for Block Play

The first step in planning for block play involves setting up and organizing a dedicated block center with plenty of space and a smooth surface for building. Low-pile carpeting works well. Children will be using the center to build and to conduct experiments. Teachers need to consider what materials to include and how to store blocks and props so children can see and access what they need to carry out their plans. With the children's input, they can set guidelines for using and caring for construction materials.

Selecting Materials

Materials in the block center need to reflect what works best for children's ages and abilities (Giles & Tunks 2013). Teachers often supplement unit blocks with other construction materials such as cardboard blocks and LEGOs, DUPLOs, or similar brands. Original LEGOs are best suited for children with developed fine motor skills, while younger children more easily manipulate DUPLO blocks. Look online to find a variety of blocks that appeal to preschoolers and to research ideas for creating blocks from recycled or repurposed materials.

Storage

A well-organized storage system helps children find specific items as they build, and makes clean-up time easier. Ample shelving for blocks and accessories is important. Display larger blocks and accessories on sturdy, open shelves. Organize smaller pieces in clear containers. Label shelves and containers with pictures and words, in English and children's home languages. In addition, make laminated copies of the unit block shapes and tape them to shelves where they are stored to help children understand where the various shapes and sizes of unit blocks are stored. This reinforces the sizes and shapes of blocks.

Guidelines for Use and Care

Clear guidelines that the children help to establish can minimize disagreements and help children concentrate on their block building. Teachers can encourage children to build in areas where structures won't be accidentally knocked over. Use tape to create a one-foot border on the floor between the block shelf and the building area. This defines the block building area and minimizes the risk of structures falling down when children reach for blocks from the shelf. Preschoolers can easily understand the benefit of building only in the designated zone.

Allowing enough time for cleanup helps children learn how to handle blocks with care. A set of simple guidelines posted in the block center reminds children of what to do. For example,

- Blocks are for building
- Keep blocks in the construction zone
- Take down only your construction

Teachers' Role in Block Play

How much teachers choose to get involved in children's block play will depend on the specific situation and the ages and abilities of the children (Chalufour & Worth 2004). The most subtle approach is to observe and record children's play and make comments such as, "I see you made two bridges using six unit blocks." More active involvement includes asking questions about children's play that help them think of alternatives. For example, a teacher might say, "I notice that you used the DUPLOs to make a walkway and then you took it apart. What else could you use to make the walkway?" The most direct way teachers might get involved is by physically assisting or even taking part in the block play. Teachers also may be directly involved to help resolve a conflict or to model how to clean up the area. Common dilemmas during block play that may require teacher intervention include children fighting over blocks, structures being accidentally knocked down, and children resisting cleaning up after block play (Tunks 2009).

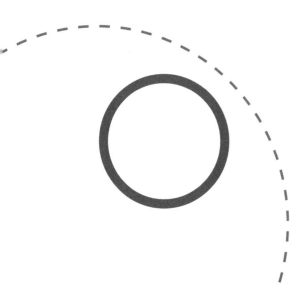

Meaningful Learning Through Block Play

Through building together, children learn to share, take turns, and collaborate in meaningful ways. Construction play also provides opportunities for children to learn problem solving, math, science, and language skills.

Math Concepts

As preschoolers manipulate blocks, they develop a deeper understanding of space and the relationships between objects. This type of learning helps children master skills such as counting, sorting, classifying, and identifying shapes. These skills form the foundation on which mathematical processes are learned. Here are some ways that teachers can use the block area to reinforce math concepts with preschoolers.

- Ask preschoolers to count the number of blocks used to build a tower. They can record their findings on paper attached to a clipboard.
- Work with the children to measure the height of a structure using standard and non-standard tools. For example, they could use a measuring tape or yardstick or they could use string, plastic links, or Unifix cubes (small interlocking cubes that help children learn about measurement).
- Use math vocabulary to compare shapes of the blocks with preschoolers. "This double unit is twice as long as the half unit." "That block is curved and this block is straight." "What other differences do you notice?"
- Use masking tape to outline complex shapes, such as trapezoids or hexagons, on the carpet in the block center. Challenge children to use unit blocks to recreate the shapes outlined on the floor.

When preschoolers have mastered this task, explore volume and area by suggesting that children try to fit blocks together inside the shapes they have outlined. "Andre, you have used two single units and two quadruple units to make a rectangle. How many half units do you think will fit in that shape?"

Science Constructs

Children can learn scientific constructs such as *height, gravity, balance, action* and *reaction*, and *cause and effect* through block play.

- Provide cardboard tubes, lengths of PVC pipe, pool noodles cut in half length wise (they are hollow), straws, string, small boxes, table tennis balls, and toy cars so children can plan and conduct experiments.
- Offer a variety of surfaces for children to build on, such as tile, cardboard, sponges, bubble wrap, and carpet squares (Giles & Tunks 2013). Engage children in discussing the pros and cons of building on each surface.
- Ask open-ended questions as children experiment to open the door for further discoveries. "What can you use to connect these two blocks?" "What could happen if you tried to balance a block on top?"
- Invite children to notice how differently shaped blocks move when pushed down a ramp, pushed across a floor, or dropped from various heights. They can experiment to see how blocks of different shapes move. "Wow, Kelli, look at that round block roll down the ramp! I wonder how blocks with other shapes will act when placed at the top of the ramp."

Language Skills

Opportunities for using language and increasing vocabulary are a natural result of block play. Vocabulary such as *shape, number, size*, and *order* supports children's math and science learning and contributes to growth in other domains as well. Children engage in conversations, negotiate ideas as they build cooperatively, and might role-play with the block structure as the center for their play. For example, following a field trip to a firehouse, three children construct a fire station from unit blocks. They share ideas about adding accessories, including a toy fire truck, a plastic dalmatian, and a piece of surgical tubing that serves as a fire hose. They adjust the size of the fire station to accommodate the fire truck. Once complete, they put on plastic firefighter hats and become firefighters. Imagination and language energizes their play. Next, they build a house from spare blocks so they can rush into action to save lives and put out fires.

Conclusion

Unit blocks have enjoyed a long and rich history in early childhood education. The many different ways that preschoolers play with blocks makes them one of the most versatile toys in an average preschool classroom. By rethinking the block area and making some small changes, teachers can make the most of block play with pre-schoolers.

REFERENCES

Chalufour, I., & K. Worth. 2004. *Building Structures With Young Children*. St. Paul, MN: Redleaf; Washington, DC: NAEYC.

Giles, R., & K. Tunks. 2013. "Building Young Scientists: Developing Scientific Literacy Through Construction Play." *Early Years: Journal of the Texas Association for the Education of Young Children* 34 (2): 22–27.

Tunks, K.W. 2009. "Block Play: Practical Suggestions for Common Dilemmas." *Dimensions of Early Childhood* 37 (1): 3–8.

Block Type	Features
Cardboard blocks	• Large size of blocks makes it easy for small hands to grasp • Bright colors • Light, so if a tower tumbles no one will get hurt • Easy to stack • Crush resistant • Sets include varied sizes and colors
DUPLOs	• Slightly larger than LEGOs • Easier for young children to put together and pull apart
Waffle blocks	• Waffle-shaped plastic pieces that snap together • Bright colors in various sizes
Bristle blocks	• Soft, flexible interlocking plastic bristles are used to connect blocks • Can be attached to 6" x 7" building plate • Bright colors
Foam building blocks	• Multicolored blocks in various shapes and sizes • Chunky foam pieces are easy to grip

Block Type	Features
Large interlocking blocks	• Flexible plastic pieces in four shapes • Rectangular shape measures 4.5" x 9" • Durable and washable
Soft unit blocks	• Built to the same scale as unit blocks • Made of dense foam • Lightweight, colorful, and safe if thrown
Building bricks	• 2" plastic cubes that snap together • Made of bright, colorful plastic
Large hollow blocks	• Wooden blocks • Used to make child-size structures such as forts • Five different sizes and shapes, plus boards
Tabletop building blocks	• Variety of shapes • Smaller version of unit blocks • May be natural wood or wood painted bright colors
LEGOs	• Bright colors • Small, interlocking pieces • Support fine motor skills

Math and Manipulatives Learning Center

Laura J. Colker

What Children Do and Learn

Math

- Play lotto games with picture cards.
- String beads in a repeating sequence, like one yellow bead and two blue ones.
- Sort rubber dinosaurs.
- Put together puzzles.
- Place pegs in a pegboard.
- Play with magnetic numbers.
- Stretch rubber bands on a geoboard.
- Build with connecting blocks.
- Place blocks with geometric shapes on parquetry pattern cards.
- Arrange Cuisenaire rods.
- Make graphs.

Language and Literacy

- Learn vocabulary in English and home languages (*manipulatives; construction; graph; magnetic; counter*).
- Put together an alphabet puzzle.
- Read books about math concepts.
- Return materials to their place on shelves.
- Make signs for their constructions.

Physical

- Use lacing or buttoning frames.
- Thread laces through holes on sewing cards.

Setup Tips

- Locate near the classroom entrance. This offers a quiet and engaging activity at drop-off or pickup times.
- Provide a table where four to six children can sit and work, but be sure to have space to work on the floor as well.
- Make sure that signs and books in the area are in English and children's home languages.
- Invite family volunteers to play a board game or put together a floor puzzle with several children.
- Ask families what materials their children enjoy playing with at home. "Do you enjoy playing color bingo or lotto games?"

Budget Stretchers

- Create a lotto game featuring photos of the children laminated on index cards. With a duplicate set of photos, children can match their friends' faces.
- Find board games and puzzles at yard sales and thrift stores.
- Look to nature for manipulatives to sort and categorize—shells, acorns, leaves, pebbles, and the like.

Beyond the Basics

- Offer library books on architecture to inspire children to make interesting and innovative constructions.
- Encourage children to use the materials in unexpected ways—for example, parquetry blocks as stencils rather than patterning pieces.
- Help children develop math skills using all kinds of manipulatives. Children can count the stitches on a lacing frame or order the steps involved in using a zipper frame. They can make patterns on a sewing card and embroider different shapes. Children can discover math anywhere and everywhere.

Include Children's Families and Cultures

- Include books, signs, and labels in both English and children's home languages.
- Encourage families to bring in familiar objects from home that may serve as manipulatives in the center. For example, families may choose to share loose buttons, seashells from a recent trip to the beach, or muffin tins to use for sorting.

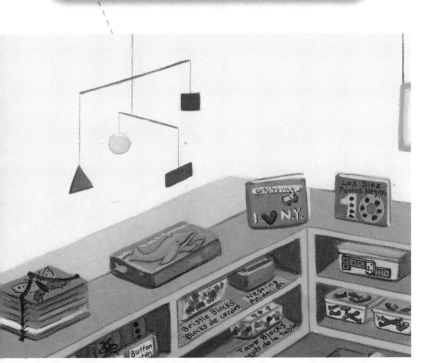

Mimi's Marble Maze
Laberinto de canicas

Raul's roller coaster game
Juego de la montaña rusa

Craft Foam
Espuma para artesanías

Rubber Bands
Bandas de goma

Velcro

Paste
Pegamento

Glue
Goma de pega

Goodly Eyes
Ojos artificiales

Sand Timers
Relojes de arena

Pegs
Clavijas

Marbles
Canicas

Tape
Cinta

Hand Drill
Taladro manual

Magnetic Cloth
Tela magnética

Place Keepers and Spinners
Fichas y ruletas

Magazines
Revistas

Wooden Puzzle Peices
Rompecabezas de madera

Cardboard Blocks
Bloques de cartón

Construction Paper
Cartulina

Cat Puzzle

Our Class Lo
Juego de lotería

Felt
Fieltro

A Place for Making Games and Puzzles

Laura J. Colker

A place for making games and puzzles, housed in the math and manipulatives learning center, offers children the chance to use their creativity to invent games and puzzles they and their peers can play with.

Materials—Children can use many different types of materials to make games and puzzles. Some possibilities include dice, dominoes, cardboard, scissors, marbles, rubber bands, and materials to decorate the games. Teachers may also want to keep the center stocked with books about games and making games and trays so that children can easily transport their work.

Games and Puzzles

Picture puzzle: Draw a picture (or choose a photo) and glue it onto a piece of cardboard. Wait until the glue is completely dry—this may take a day or so. Then cut the picture into puzzle pieces.

Matching game: Use 6-10 index cards to make a simple matching game. Paint an image on one index card. Before the paint dries, place a blank index card on top of the painted one. Press down, and pull the index cards apart. Do this until you reach the desired amount of cards. Once the paint dries, play the game by putting all of the cards face down, and try to find the matching pairs by flipping over one card at a time.

Ring toss: Tape a paper towel roll to the center of a paper plate to make a post. Cut the center out of 5-8 paper plates to serve as "rings." Feel free to decorate the stand or rings. To play the game, players stand three feet away from the post and try to toss the rings around the post or onto the stand.

What Children Do and Learn

Math
- Make patterns of holes on a wood board using a hand drill.
- Make and play dominoes.
- Make and play lotto games based on shapes.

Physical
- Use a drill to make peg holes.
- Glue dots on foam cubes.
- Use markers and crayons to decorate materials.

Language and Literacy
- Look at books that feature puzzles, such as *Apple, Apple, Alligator*, by William Accorsi, to find ideas.
- Work with teachers to write words on games, make game pieces, and make signs.

Setup Tips

- Use a place with room for both a work table and floor space. Some children prefer to work on the floor.
- Place shelving flush to the table so children can easily reach materials.
- Use baskets to store loose supplies like crayons, markers, and felt. Store scissors separately.

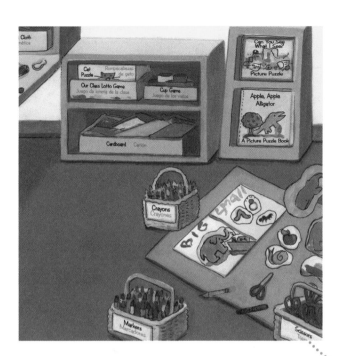

Budget Stretchers

- Use recycled cardboard from boxes and packaging.
- Ask families for materials such as felt scraps and old board games. Then collect game pieces, spinners, and sand timers.
- Check out dollar stores and yard sales for games and wooden puzzles that children can turn into new items.

Include Children's Families and Cultures

- Ask families to email you photos of their children, alone and with family members. You can enlarge and print the photos to use in puzzles and games.
- Ask families to suggest games from their culture. Invite them to share examples that inspire children to make similar ones.
- Send home instructions and materials for making simple games. Families can work with their child to create or enjoy a game or puzzle at home.

You Can Count on Math

Laura J. Colker

Every day, all day, indoors and outdoors, preschool children learn about numbers, shapes, measuring, patterns, and graphing. Daily routines, planned learning experiences, and play time all provide opportunities for teaching and learning math skills.

Number Concepts

Children begin to learn about numbers by handling concrete objects, putting these real things into all sorts of relationships, and comparing quantities. With experience, preschoolers learn to count and identify numerals by name; they understand that the number "3" stands for three objects.

Ways to Teach Preschoolers About Number Concepts

Ask questions throughout the day: "How many are there?" "How many are left?" "How can we figure out how many we need?"

Sing counting songs and finger plays: When children sing songs such as "Five Little Monkeys Jumping on the Bed," they are learning about counting. "Five little monkeys jumping on the bed, one fell off and bumped his head. Mama called the doctor and the doctor said, 'No more monkeys jumping on the bed!' Four little monkeys jumping on the bed . . ."

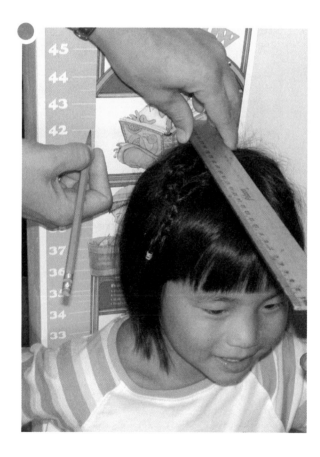

Invite children to count: In the library area, for example, children can count the number of books about nature, puppets in the basket, or chairs at the writing table. At snack time they can count to see if there are enough graham crackers for each child to have one.

Offer a variety of materials for exploring number concepts: Board games that use dice, ingredients on recipe cards, counting books, and tapes or CDs featuring counting songs and finger plays.

Explore one-to-one correspondence: By putting one plate and one napkin at each place, this child is linking one—and only one!—number name to an object. He is building the foundation for counting.

Geometry and Spatial Sense

Geometry is the study of shape and size. Preschool children need lots of practice handling shapes to understand what makes a circle a circle and a square a square. Spatial sense includes being aware of one's own position (*on, off, behind, in front of*) and distance (*near, far, next to*) in relation to other people and objects.

Ways to Teach Preschoolers About Geometry and Spatial Sense

Talk about shapes: "Look at the hole. It's a round circle. There are lots of circles in this pegboard."

Talk about space: Use words about space as they occur naturally during play: "You are standing under the tree branch." "Mary is crawling *through* the hoops." "Ramon stepped *over* the rock."

Invite children to make body shapes: Ask two or three children to hold hands to make a circle. Have them use their legs to form triangles, squares, or diamonds. This gives them a feel for how space affects shapes.

Offer a variety of materials for exploring geometry and spatial sense: Include shape sponges, shape cookie cutters, wooden beads, attribute blocks, puzzles, and books on shapes.

Invite children to explore shapes and spaces: While building with unit blocks, children can explore the characteristics of three-dimensional shapes;

matching the blocks to shape labels on shelves during cleanup teaches shapes and spatial orientation. Work with children to construct and use a maze with hollow blocks. Make a map of the outdoor area showing the play equipment, snack table, and garden or map out whose cot or mat goes where during rest time.

Measurement

Measurement is used to observe and record information about the height, weight, length, or depth of people and things. "How tall am I?" "How much does Fluffy the cat weigh?" "How deep is that hole?" Before learning to use standard measurement tools like rulers and tape measures, preschoolers can explore and compare measurement traits (height, width) using familiar objects or nonstandard measuring tools (like crayons).

Ways to Teach Preschoolers About Measurement

Introduce comparison vocabulary: Use words such as *longer, heavier, wider, taller, lighter* in everyday conversations.

Use timers for taking turns: "When the timer goes off, you can use the computer." Experiencing how time passes helps children begin to understand concepts and words related to standard time measurements— seconds, minutes, hours.

Provide opportunities to measure: Children can measure ingredients for a recipe, the length of a jump, the size of a cubby, their heights and weights, the height of plants growing in the garden, or the length of a shadow.

Point out nonstandard measuring tools: Children can measure using pieces of yarn or string, hardwood unit blocks, shoes, belts, the side of a book, a stuffed animal, or body parts, such as hands and feet. Play with nonstandard measurements by asking questions such as "How many crayons wide is each butterfly?"

Comparison: "My head comes up to your shoulder." Making comparisons is a basic part of measurement.

Patterns

A pattern is a regularly repeated arrangement of numbers, objects, events, shapes, sizes, colors, or musical notes. It can be found in a design (three round sphere blue beads followed by two yellow cubes) or a physical activity (two short claps followed by one long clap). At the preschool level, the focus is on what makes up a pattern. In kindergarten and the primary grades, children will apply this understanding to patterns in arithmetic such as odd and even numbers or counting by 5s and 10s.

Ways to Teach Preschoolers About Patterning

Provide opportunities to extend patterns: Children use a variety of materials to string beads, make patterns, draw shapes on paper, use shape stickers to make designs, or sing repeated refrains in songs.

Have children create their own patterns: Provide crayons, markers, paints, stickers, buttons, beads, or colored counting bears. Outside on a warm day, children can step in water and make patterns with their feet on the pavement.

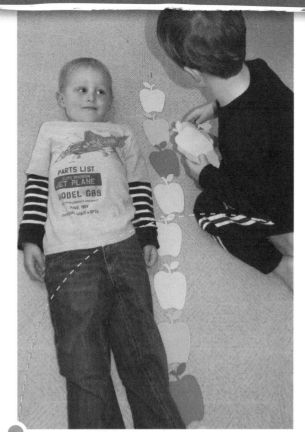

Explore patterns in the classroom and outdoors: Help children notice patterns in carpets, wallpaper, borders on posters, quilts, the daily schedule, clothing, flowers, butterflies, and other natural items.

Have children make patterns using their bodies: Invite children to sit down, stand up, and sit down several times in a row. Clap your hands fast-slow-fast-slow and have children repeat the pattern. Play Duck, Duck, Goose.

Introduce patterning through music: Using a rhythm instrument or your hands, play or clap short rhythmic patterns. Invite children to repeat and then extend the pattern. Later, make patterns longer and more complicated. Have children create their own. Sing songs and use finger plays with repeated choruses, such as "B-I-N-G-O."

Analyzing and Representing Data

Graphing is one way children can display and share information they have collected and sorted. Children can make graphs using concrete objects, pictures, or symbols.

Ways to Teach Preschoolers About Analyzing and Representing Data

Have children collect and represent data in graphs: They can collect data about who takes the bus to school, favorite foods served at lunch, children who slept at rest time, or children who helped themselves to a snack during choice time.

Provide real objects to use for graphs: Children's graphs can use items such as foods, cans, books, shoes, hats, and gloves/mittens.

Provide items to use as symbols to represent data: Offer a variety of items, such as photos of children, drawings of what's being graphed, leaves, ribbons, stamps, buttons and shape stickers, or paper cutouts of dots, triangles, or squares.

Have children sort items by attributes of their own choosing: Children can sort jackets into two groups—ones with zippers and ones without. They can separate toys that are soft from those that are hard. They can line up by the color of their clothing: red, blue, green, or yellow.

Ask questions that invite children to collect data: "How many children have freckles?" "Whose shoes have laces?" "Who has a pet?"

Books About Counting to 10 and Higher

Lauren Baker

Most preschoolers are eager to learn about numbers and what they mean. Read and talk about these counting books with children to support their developing math skills.

1-2-3 Peas, by Keith Baker. 2012. Beach Lane Books.

From the author of the bestselling alphabet book *LMNO Peas* comes a book about numbers. The fun and familiar peas count 1 through 10 and then count by tens until they reach 100. Even children who may not be ready to count by tens will enjoy the book's exciting illustrations and the lively pea characters.

One Duck Stuck, by Phyllis Root, illus. by Jane Chapman. 1998. Candlewick Press.

PLOP! PLUNK! SLOOSH! From 2 fish to 10 dragonflies, count Duck's friends as they rush to help him out of the muck. Only when they work together can they pull Duck from the marsh. The bright illustrations, animal noises, and sound effects will make this story a fast favorite.

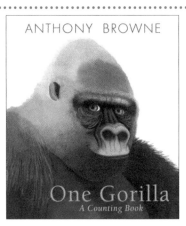

One Gorilla: A Counting Book, by Anthony Browne. 2012. Candlewick Press.

Beautifully illustrated, *One Gorilla* is memorable for its vivid and intensely detailed portraits of primates. Simplistic text offsets the incredible illustrations, drawing attention to the personalities suggested in the faces of each animal. The featured primates are distinctive and easy to count.

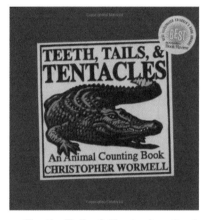

Teeth, Tails, & Tentacles: An Animal Counting Book, by Christopher Wormell. 2004. Running Press Kids.

Minimal text and crisp illustrations invite readers to count from 1 to 20 by noting animal markings, legs, claws, and eyes. The final pages offer more information about the animals from earlier pages. A newer work that feels like a classic, this concept book will inspire further thinking about math, counting, and creatures.

How many peas are in a pod? Snack time math. Continue the pea counting adventure after reading *1-2-3 Peas*. Each child can choose a pea pod, pry it open, and count how many peas are inside. Encourage the children to sort the peas by size or shape or make a graph. Once they have finished counting and sorting, they can wash and then eat the peas as a snack.

Get wild about counting! After counting animals in *One Gorilla, Teeth, Tails & Tentacles*, and *One Duck Stuck*, ask the children to count and sort plastic toy animals. They may be interested in grouping the manipulatives by type of animal or counting in sets of two or three.

Use rhythm to count and find patterns. Turn on music and clap your hands or tap your feet to the beat. Invite children to follow you in the same rhythm. Once they have found the rhythm, lead the group in counting along with the beat. Challenge the children to identify patterns in the music and notice where the beat sounds the same and where it changes.

Count and measure. Take counting work to the next level by using numbers in measurements. Have the children stack towers of LEGO blocks to measure objects around the room. They can count how many blocks tall or wide an object is. Use LEGO and DUPLO blocks to measure the children's height. Encourage the children to talk together and compare their findings.

Using Children's Books to Introduce Math Terms

Sarah Normandie

Why do this activity? Learning about numbers is more than just learning to count and recognize numerals. Through hands-on experiences children can explore the quantity each number represents and explore concepts like size and quantity.

      What can children learn? Children understand new mathematical terms, specifically the phrases *more than, less than*, and *equal to*. They also learn how to count, estimate, and compare representational numbers ("3" or "three") with the physical number in objects (holding three beanbags).

Vocabulary words: *more than, less than, the same as*

Materials:

- *Ten Apples Up On Top!* by Dr. Seuss
- At least 10 small beanbags
- A quiet space in the classroom

Prepare for the Activity

1. As a whole group, read the book *Ten Apples Up On Top!* by Dr. Seuss to the children. Pay special attention to math terms and phrases—such as *more than*—as they come up in the story.
2. Designate an area of the room where the activity will take place and set out the beanbags gathered for this activity. Make sure that the area has space for your group to stand, sit, and move around freely.

Lead Small Groups

1. Before you begin the activity, ask the children what they can remember about the book *Ten Apples Up On Top!* You may want to ask them questions about the characters, the contest that the characters participate in, and how this competition ends. If the children have a hard time remembering the story, review it with them before you begin the activity.
2. After talking about the book and the competition that the characters of the book find themselves participating in, challenge preschoolers to imitate the characters in the book by balancing beanbag "apples" on top of their heads. First count the beanbags on your own, one child at a time. Next work with the children to count the beanbags. Then have the children count them on their own.
3. Next compare the numbers of beanbags the children have. After you've counted the beanbags prompt the children with questions. Begin by asking, "Who has more?" "Who has less?" and "Who has the same amount?" The children are likely to answer the questions and laugh as beanbags fall off their heads and will be eager to try again.
4. Finally ask the children to take the beanbags off of their heads. Have the children take the role of the teacher and start coming up with numbers to use in this comparison game. Help the children by teaching them to check their work by counting the beanbags one at a time after they answer questions comparing how many beanbags each child has. Encourage them to use mathematical language—such as *more than, less than, the same as*—when answering the questions the children and teachers ask them.

Respond to Individual Needs

1. Place the beanbags and book on a table in the class-room for the next few weeks. Children can revisit the familiar book and practice their balancing and counting skills on their own and with friends and partners during center time.

2. Introduce vocabulary words in English and in the children's home languages. Use the words to de-scribe the number of beanbags that children have.

Follow Up After the Activity

1. Use the phrases *more than, less than,* and *the same as* regularly in conversations with preschoolers. For example a teacher might note, "There are more peo-ple playing in the block center than are playing in the science center."

2. Compare amounts of other objects children see as a part of their day. For example a teacher might say "I wonder if we have more trucks stored outdoors or indoors." After the children find an answer, teachers can work with children to check their work together by counting how many are stored inside and how many trucks are stored outside.

Involve Families

1. Announce the activity in a family newsletter or on a bulletin board. Explain how families can use math vocabulary such as *more than* and *less than* in their daily activities—such as at the supermarket.

2. Take photos of the children doing this activity to email to families, share on social media, or post on the program's website.

3. Encourage families to play this simple comparison game at home. Families can work with children to compare settings at the dinner table, books on the book shelf, or any number of materials they have around the house.

Preschoolers Getting in Shape

Julie Sarama and Douglas H. Clements

Why do this activity? Children build their ideas about shapes by actively manipulating them. This can involve moving shapes with their hands or tracing the borders of the shapes with their eyes. Yet even if children can name shapes, their knowledge may be limited. Some children may not really understand the concept of a square if they cannot explore an unseen square with their hands and then name the shape correctly.

What can children learn? Children will understand what basic shapes look and feel like. They will also know and use their own definitions of shapes to decide if any figure is a member of that shape class or not (Spitler, Sarama, & Clements 2003). They develop independent thinking and positive attitudes toward learning and applying mathematics.

Vocabulary words: *angle, circle, plane, polygon, rectangle, right angle, rhombus, square, side, triangle*

Materials:

- Feely box
- Small shapes to put inside the feely box

Prepare for the Activity

1. Create a feely box. Feely boxes can be made in different ways. Our favorite is a box with two holes on opposite sides and cloth tubes attached to each hole to prevent peeking. The two holes allow children to use both hands to explore the shape inside the box.

2. Designate an area of the room where the activity will take place and set out the feely box. Make sure that the area has space for your group to stand, sit, and move around freely.

Lead Small Groups

1. At first, children focus on matching hidden shapes to shapes they can see. Gather two identical sets of a few (three to six) different shapes. Place one set out of sight and secretly place one shape of this set in the freely box. Show the out of sight set to children. One child puts his hand in the box to feel the shape and then points to the matching shape on display. He then removes the hidden shape to check his accuracy.

2. Next children will conceptualize the shape they are feeling, state the name of the shape, and describe its attributes. In this second activity, no shapes are displayed. Children are challenged to feel the shapes and name them. They then explain how they figured it out. For example, a child might say, "Three sides—three straight sides! It's a triangle!"

3. Finally, children must understand and describe the shapes' attributes without naming it. Again, there are no displays. One child feels and then describes the shape. The goal is for the child to *describe* the shape so well that other children can figure out the shape and name it. Children then explain how they knew which shape their friend was describing. One small group had this conversation:

> **Mari:** It's got right angles.
>
> **Daniel:** A rectangle!
>
> **Mari:** Wait! Um ... all sides are the same, like the same as each other.
>
> **Lukas:** A rhombus! A rhombus.
>
> **Mari:** Yeah, but it's ummm ... a special shape with all right angles.
>
> **Daniel, Lukas, and Ada:** A square!
>
> **Mari:** Right! Look [pulls out the square].

Respond to Individual Needs

Teachers can ask these questions to help children think about this math activity.

1. "What words can you use to tell me what you are feeling?"
2. "Are the lines straight or curved?"
3. "What kind of shape could it be?"
4. "What kind of shape could it not be?"
5. "What patterns do you notice in the room?"

Follow Up After the Activity

1. Allow time for children to observe and discuss the shapes in the feely box together and with their families. This can be done during drop-off and pick-up times, or whenever the children have a free-play opportunity.
2. Place books about shapes in the library area. Some books preschoolers might enjoy include *Perfect Square* by Michael Hall and *Shape by Shape* by Susie MacDonald.

Involve Families

Write a set of directions telling families how they can make a feely box at home. Send it to families in a newsletter, email, or on your program's website. Include a quick summary of some of the ways that children have been using the feely box at school, including the shape guessing game.

REFERENCE

Spitler, M.E., J. Sarama, & D.H. Clements. 2003. "A Preschooler's Understanding of 'Triangle:' A Case Study." Paper presented at the 81st Annual Meeting of the National Council of Teachers of Mathematics, San Antonio, TX.

Everyday Math Manipulatives

Meghan Dombrink-Green

Manipulatives are small items preschoolers can use to sort, categorize, count, measure, match, and make patterns. They can then show their discoveries in graphs and drawings. Teachers can use manipulatives to create math games that introduce concepts such as one-to-one correspondence—using one counting word for each object. From bear counters to dominoes, there are many manipulatives teachers can buy. But there are also many free or low-cost items that work just as well (be sure they are clean before adding them to the classroom). Here are eight everyday materials that work well as math manipulatives.

1 Stones

Collect stones while taking a nature walk with the children. If you are visiting a park, make sure it is okay to remove natural items.

2 Balls

Collect balls in different sizes, materials, and colors. Look for bouncy rubber balls, golf balls, tennis balls, stress balls, racquetballs, foam balls, pom-poms, or other small round items.

3 Shells

Many families collect shells on a trip to the beach. Check them for sharp edges. You can also look online for companies that sell inexpensive bags of shells.

7 Cardboard tubes

Save the tubes from paper towel, plastic wrap, and wrapping paper rolls and cut into smaller pieces. Recycle larger cardboard tubes used to mail posters, or purchase at office supply stores.

8 Bottle caps and lids

Start a new habit—save plastic caps from milk jugs, detergent bottles, single-serve containers, dish-washing soap, and shampoo bottles. Save the lids from food containers like yogurt cups, applesauce jars, and cream cheese tubs.

4 Buttons

Buttons come in many shapes, sizes, and colors. Children can also sort them by number of holes.

5 Coffee stirrers

Wood and plastic coffee stirrers come in different lengths and colors. Cut them to make shorter lengths. Purchase them or collect donations from gas stations, coffee shops, or other local businesses.

6 Keys

Invite families to provide unused keys for your collection. For more variety, ask a local locksmith or hardware store if they have extra keys to give to your class.

Tips for Using Math Manipulatives

- Organize the objects in clearly labeled tubs, plastic zipper bags, baskets, boxes, or plastic containers.
- Provide ice cube trays, egg cartons, and muffin tins for sorting activities.
- Introduce math vocabulary that children can use to talk about what they are doing (*circle, rectangle, longer than, shorter than, pattern, estimate, size, measure, texture, analyze, graph*).

Sorting Activities for Preschoolers

William C. Ritz

I magine a supermarket where goods are arranged alphabetically, where a single aisle displays everything from lemons to light bulbs to liver! Most of us would find it difficult to shop for what we need in such a store. Fortunately, grocers arrange products into sensible and familiar categories that make shopping easy.

In our everyday lives, we often arrange objects, ideas, and events into convenient groups or categories. Early experiences in sorting things into groups help young learners to better observe how things are alike and different—essential early literacy and math skills. Preschools typically have a variety of materials on hand that children can sort in different ways, and most preschoolers will do so with little encouragement. Becoming increasingly skilled at sorting helps learners of all ages to cope with all the information around us in the modern world.

Mommy's Button Box

Years ago, my mother kept a box filled with spare buttons. If you lost a button, she would search the button box to find the best match. A collection of buttons of different shapes, colors, sizes, and materials can also be a wonderful resource for preschool learners. (*Caution*: Remind children not to put buttons in their mouths, as they are a choking hazard!)

Gather a small group of five or six children and provide individual sectioned containers, such as egg cartons or ice cube trays, and plastic magnifiers. Invite each child to select 10 to 15 buttons of various shapes, colors, sizes, and materials. Encourage the children to examine the buttons and describe how they are alike and how they are different. Invite the children to use the magnifiers to make more detailed observations about the designs of the buttons.

Next, challenge the children to put buttons of the same color, size, or design into the container sections. Explain that this is called *sorting*. Ask open-ended questions that lead children to explain why they grouped their buttons in a particular way. After children have sorted their buttons one way, suggest that they empty the containers to pile the buttons together again. Say, "Now you can sort your buttons again. How do you want to sort them this time?" Ask the children to describe why they have chosen to sort the buttons as they have. Point out that any sorting choice is okay; there is no one correct way.

When the children become familiar with the task, encourage them to sort other objects as well—shapes, coins, seeds, beads, and so on.

Math

A *set* is a collection of objects considered as a whole—a collection of things that share a particular property (such as the same color). When children sort objects, they are creating sets (and often subsets too). The concept of sets is important in mathematics. To support children's early experiences in sorting, use the word *set* frequently to help preschoolers build a foundation for future understanding and use of this concept: "Olivia, show George your set of blue bottle caps."

Provide children with cardboard or wooden geometric shapes. Suggest that they sort the shapes into groups. If the collection contains shapes of different colors, children can sort by color as well as shape. Remember, however, that preschoolers first learn to sort by only one characteristic at a time.

Art

Plan a leaf-pressing activity using wax paper and a warm iron. Be sure to work in small groups and supervise closely. Hang groups of finished pressings with similar properties (for example, all of the oak leaves) in one place as colorful transparencies in sunlit windows.

Use buttons from the button box to create free-form collages on construction paper or in boxes. Children might use buttons to make designs or flower shapes. They might use buttons of one color for the stem and buttons of another color for petals.

Buttons can be turned into interesting accessories. Using string or dental floss, children can thread sorted buttons, for example, alternating buttons with different characteristics to create necklaces, key chains, or bracelets.

Curriculum Connections

Sorting activities connect easily with other areas of the curriculum. Here are a few examples of curriculum connections teachers and children can explore.

Science and Nature

Take the children for a walk to collect leaves from different kinds of trees and with different colors. Encourage them to examine the leaves to find interesting characteristics. Talk about differences and similarities. "What other leaves are like this one?" "Are all the leaves from one kind of tree the same size?" "The same color?" Ask the children to sort the leaves by similar characteristics: size, color, shape, and so on. Encourage children to re-sort leaves several different ways, based on a variety of traits.

Reading

Include these children's books related to sorting or classifying in learning centers:

Agrupemos alimentos (2002), by Patricia Whitehouse

Aunt Ippy's Museum of Junk (1991), by Rodney Greenblat

Let's Sort (2003), by David Bauer. Also available as *Vamos a clasificar* (2005)

Make a Match: A Preschool Sorting Game (2006), by Tish Rabe, illus. by Mary Anne Lloyd

Sorting and Sets (2006), by Henry Arthur Pluckrose

Sorting Through Spring (2013), by Lizann Flatt, illus. by Ashley Barron

Alike or Not Alike: A Photo Sorting Game (2012), by Kristen McCurry

Sorting by Color (2007), by Jennifer L. Marks

Supporting Dual Language Learners

Because sorting is a way of making sense of the world around us it can be especially helpful for young dual language learners (DLLs). To get the greatest benefit from these activities, connect the sorting items with other areas of interest in the classroom. Sort buttons when reading *Corduroy* with the children. Change the sorting supplies to small metallic and non-metallic items when the children have been exploring with magnets. Sort real leaves or pebbles they recognize and have collected from their neighborhood. With these connections, DLLs have the words to participate with each activity. They can focus on the features of the items and the activity of sorting when they are using items they know and can talk about in English or in their home language.

Developing Math Games Based on Children's Books

Kay M. Cutler, Deanna Gilkerson, Sue Parrott, and Mary Teresa Bowne

Creating board games based on well-loved children's books is one way to encourage preschoolers to develop and use math skills. While playing board games, children can explore matching, one-to-one correspondence (as when a child gives each player one game piece), counting, and more. Many children's books provide natural, meaningful ways for children to explore math concepts. Some books have built-in math content, while in others the story line sets the stage for a board game.

Supplies for making games are inexpensive and easy to find.

- **Game board:** Use tagboard, foam core board, or old game boards covered with contact paper.
- **Spinners and dice:** Make your own to match children's math skills. For example, use a small block of wood to make a die with dots and numerals indicating one to three for younger preschoolers. Make a spinner with dots and matching numerals.
- **Game pieces:** Look at craft shops and discount stores. Online vendors such as Oriental Trading or U.S. Toy Company offer a variety of unusual items.

Here are descriptions of a few board games based on favorite children's books. The games appear in order of difficulty, starting with lotto games, the easiest to play.

Inch by Inch, by Leo Lionni. 1960. New York: HarperCollins.

A smart inchworm talks a robin out of eating him by offering to measure the robin's tail. He measures other items for the birds, until a nightingale asks the inchworm to measure his song.

Type of game: Circular path

What children learn: Numbers, measurement

Preparation: Make a game board using a 16" x 20" piece of tagboard. Draw a circular path around the board. Color eight spaces purple, evenly spread throughout the circle. Color the remaining spaces orange. Make a spinner with dots representing numbers 1 through 5. Find and print in different sizes computer images of the birds in the story (robin, nightingale, hummingbird). Use the images to make a set of cards. Make several small pipe-cleaner inchworms—all the same size. Children will use the inchworms to measure.

How to play: Children use the spinner and move their game piece the correct number of spaces. When a child lands on a purple square, he or she draws a bird card, then estimates the bird's length in inchworms. The player measures the bird using a pipe-cleaner inchworm. If the estimate is correct, the child gets to keep the card. Play continues until all the game cards are used or until children lose interest.

I Know an Old Lady Who Swallowed a Pie, by Alison Jackson, illus. by Judith B. Schachner. 2002. New York: Puffin.

A hungry, old woman comes to Thanksgiving dinner. After devouring the pie she brought to share, she continues to feast on the rest of the family's dinner.

Type of game: Lotto—picture grids with a set of matching cards

What children can learn: Matching, patterns, one-to-one correspondence

Preparation: Make individual picture grids using heavy paper. Draw lines to divide each board into nine squares. Draw or find clip-art images of the foods the old lady in the book eats (cider, pie, turkey, salad). Make multiples. Paste an image in each of the nine squares. Reproduce the same drawings or clip-art images to create a set of matching playing cards.

How to play: Give each child a grid. Stack the cards and place them facedown on the table or floor within children's reach. Players take turns drawing a card to see what food item the hungry lady will eat. Then they match the card with the image on their game board. Children play until one player has covered an entire board with matching cards.

Peter's Chair, by Ezra Jack Keats. 1967. New York: Harper & Row.

Peter is not happy about having a new baby sister. His blue furniture is being painted pink for her to use, so he takes the last unpainted item, his old chair, and runs away. But as he sits in his baby chair and begins to think, he realizes what it means to be a big brother.

Type of game: Tug-of-war: the starting space in the middle of the path; two ending spaces at either end of the path

What children learn: Numbers and numeral recognition, counting, patterns

Preparation: Create a large game board for two players. On the left side of the board, paste images of one blue chair and one pink chair. On the right side, paste a pink chair across from the blue one on the left, and a blue chair across from the pink. Place 13 dots in between each blue and pink chair. Use a different colored dot in the middle, where children will start. Create a spinner that indicates color (pink or blue) and number of spaces (one to three).

How to play: Two children play at a time. Each player has a game piece that represents Peter. Children take turns flicking the spinner and moving their Peter the correct number of spaces toward the color chair the spinner indicates. Children continue to play until each reaches a chair and "decides" which color Peter will paint his sister's chair.

Corduroy, by Don Freeman. 1968. New York: Viking.

A stuffed bear wanders around a toy store late at night looking for his lost button. But when he tries to pull a button off a mattress, he accidentally knocks over a lamp, alerting the night watchman, who places him back on the shelf. The next day, a little girl buys him and gives him a new button and a new home.

Type of game: Short path (10 to 20 spaces)

What children learn: Numbers and numeral recognition, counting, patterns

Preparation: Create a game board with four short paths using bear paw prints as spaces. At the beginning of each path, paste a red, yellow, blue, or green paper square (use a different color for each path). At the end

of the path, paste a button. Make two spinners: one with numbers 1 through 4 and another with bears of two sizes. Use plastic bears (two sizes) as the pieces.

How to play: There are two ways children can play this game. For both versions, the goal is to find each bear's button at the end of the path.

1. Each child begins by placing a colored plastic bear on the matching color square. Children take turns using the number spinner (or rolling a die) and moving their bear the correct number of spaces.

2. Each player has two bears—one small and one large. On each turn, children use both spinners to see which bear to move and how many spaces to move the bear.

Make Way for Ducklings, by Robert McCloskey. 1941. New York: Viking.

With the help of a police officer, Mr. and Mrs. Mallard return to their home in the Boston Public Garden with their eight children.

Type of game: Long path (such as in Candyland)

What children learn: Number and operations, patterns, algebra

Preparation: Create a game board with a long path. Alongside the path, add pictures of people or obstacles (such as the river, Officer Michael, cars, and the bridge over the pond) that the Mallards face in the order they occur in the book. You will need a spinner or die.

How to play: The goal of this game is to help Mrs. Mallard move her ducklings safely from the river to the city park. Children roll the die or use the spinner and move their game piece the correct number of spaces. Children can tell and retell the story using the game board: "Where did the ducklings go first?" "Then what did they do?" "Who or what did they see next?"

Supporting Dual Language Learners

Developing math games based on familiar children's books is a great activity that has additional benefits for dual language learners (DLLs). When children are learning to make sense of new words in English, they need multiple opportunities to hear and say those words in different contexts. By combining the story with the game, DLLs practice important math skills and reinforce key vocabulary from the book. Whenever you introduce new skills, it is best to use familiar materials and words so DLLs can build on their prior knowledge and proceed with confidence. Reading the story and then using it to create a math game is like building a learning bridge for the DLLs in your class.

Making Math Games

- Choose a book based on math concepts that children are ready to learn or because the book's story line and content can be linked to math.
- Consider the target players' ages and developmental levels.
- Choose the type of game (lotto and short path games are best for young children).
- Create a flexible game. Think of ways to make the game grow with the children. Include features that help children learn more than one concept while playing.
- Make your board and game pieces sturdy so they will last a long time.

To Make Games More Challenging

- Provide two spinners or two dice. Watch as children figure out how to move the total number of spaces represented by the two numerals.
- Create cards with extra steps. Have children take one at the beginning of each turn.
- Have children perform additional steps if they land on particular spaces on the board.

Math and Manipulatives Learning Center Checklist

Laura J. Colker

 You can complete this checklist for the math and manipulatives learning center in your classroom on your own or with a teaching colleague. When you are finished, review the items you rated as "rarely" and create an action plan to help change the rating to "sometimes" or "regularly."

	Regularly	Sometimes	Rarely
1. Children choose to play in the math and manipulatives center every day.	○	○	○
2. Children know and follow the rules for the math and manipulatives center.	○	○	○
3. The center is located away from louder areas, such as the music and movement center.	○	○	○
4. Materials are stored in labeled containers and shelves within children's reach.	○	○	○
5. There are books about math and mathematicians.	○	○	○
6. Children can save their constructions and complete them later.	○	○	○
7. Children have fun and express pleasure in playing with math and manipulatives.	○	○	○
8. While playing in the math and manipulatives center, children can express thoughts and feelings and build skills in all domains.	○	○	○
9. The math center has			
• Self-correcting, structured toys like puzzles, self-help frames, and nesting cups	○	○	○
• Open-ended toys like LEGOs, sewing cards, magnetic letters and numbers, and parquetry blocks	○	○	○
• Collectibles like keys, bottle caps, and buttons	○	○	○
• Group games like lotto, dominoes, and board games	○	○	○
10. Teachers extend children's play by			
• Asking questions	○	○	○
• Offering ideas	○	○	○
• Commenting on children's explorations and creations	○	○	○
• Providing new props that offer different experiences and challenges	○	○	○

Science

Exploring Motion

Elizabeth A. Sherwood and Amy Freshwater

Today, all states and the District of Columbia have early learning standards or guidelines that define what preschool children should know and be able to learn. Typically early learning standards address intellectual, language, physical, social, and emotional development. "By defining the desired content and outcomes of young children's education, early learning standards can lead to greater opportunities for positive development and learning in these early years" (NAEYC & NAECS/SDE 2002).

This article describes how teachers can use engaging, developmentally appropriate experiences to ensure that children have many opportunities to meet early learning standards.

Getting Started: Early Planning

As teacher educators, we wanted to investigate science in the early childhood classroom. We came up with two questions related to early learning standards for science.

1. How can teachers use science standards to support learning in ways that are developmentally appropriate, meaningful, and fun?
2. How can children achieve science benchmarks (descriptions of skills, knowledge, and performance appropriate for preschoolers) while exploring science concepts?

To answer these questions, we partnered with a preschool teacher, Stephanie. Together we would apply the standards to a familiar classroom activity—marble painting.

First, we reviewed all areas of state and national early learning standards to consider what children might learn from marble painting. Next, we created a planning web to identify the many ways marble painting can enrich and enhance learning. We thought of ideas the children might have and activities we could introduce. We wondered, How can children make marble paintings bigger or smaller? What vocabulary can they learn while doing this activity?

We also hoped the children would figure things out using *scientific inquiry* (the diverse ways children learn about and understand the natural world). They could solve problems about position and motion as they made their marble paintings. And they could learn ways to tell others about their discoveries.

What Did the Children Already Know?

The preschoolers in Stephanie's class were very familiar with marble painting. Four-year-old Karli gave clear directions as she picked up a paint-spattered box lid: "Put in a piece of paper. Put in a marble from the paint and roll it around. Hold the box and tip it." She knew the steps in the process, where to place the marbles, and how to move them. Karli had a simple understanding of the basics of gravity and force.

Three-year-old Teon also understood the process, saying, "It rolls. It gets paint on. It makes little lines where the ball goes."

Talking with children as they do an activity, such as marble painting, helps them make sense of information and describe what they are observing. Teachers can examine their paintings and ask children ques-

tions to support exploration and learning. For example, Stephanie said, "The blue line goes straight to the corner of the paper, then it turns and goes to this side. I wonder what happened?" Teon gestured with his hands to indicate tilting the box. Another child said, "You have to move the box every way." Stephanie summarized, "So when you move the box up on this side, the marble will roll . . . ?" "Down," the children chorused. Both children understood the cause-and-effect relationship between moving the box and moving the marble. They also knew how to control the direction of the marble's movement.

Building Communication Skills

Communication is key in supporting scientific learning. It is a basic science process skill. Communication is most effective when a teacher asks only a few questions at a time and gives the children time to think. This approach tells children, "I am really interested in what you have to say. Your ideas are important."

Teachers can encourage children to express their ideas in their own ways. Karli talked about her ideas, but Teon, at age 3, used only a few words and gestures to communicate what he knew. At times he said, "I'll show you," and did so without saying anything else. To support a child like Teon, teachers can describe his experiences out loud, modeling relevant vocabulary.

It's important to listen patiently to all young scientists. Ask for clarification, show genuine interest in and acceptance of what children say, and encourage them to use more precise language. These teaching strategies change marble painting from a simple art activity into a science exploration.

Asking open-ended questions allows children to

reflect and talk about science concepts in more complex ways. Close-ended questions, such as "What color is this?," have one right answer. Open-ended questions can have many right answers. Teachers need to practice asking open-ended questions throughout the day. They should also wait quietly to give children a chance to process the information before continuing.

Here are some examples of starter phrases that lead to open-ended questions.

"I wonder . . ."

"Why do you think?"

"Describe what you see . . ."

"What does it look like?"

"How does that happen?"

"Why did it work that way?"

"What about this part?"

"How can you tell?"

"How is this different?"

To plan open-ended questions related to marble painting, we had to understand each child's developmental level and interests. A question that supported one child's divergent thinking (coming up with many ideas) might not support another child with different abilities and interests.

When asking open-ended questions, it is essential for teachers to accept and value children's answers, even when they differ from those of older children and adults. For preschoolers, it is more important to be thoughtful than correct. Documenting a child's comments and understandings can provide useful information for assessments and for planning additional experiences that build on children's knowledge and skills.

How Could We Expand Children's Explorations and Learning?

For several days, the children had many opportunities to paint with marbles. To expand their thinking, we asked, "How could you make bigger lines?" The children thought and then responded, "We need bigger balls!" We searched the classroom and playground and found various balls used for golf, Ping-Pong, tennis, and more. As the children painted using balls of different sizes and textures, we recorded their comments. "Ooh, fuzzy," "Look, dots," and "When it tips, they all go down." The children's comments showed they were paying close attention to details—a part of science inquiry.

The children had noticed that dropping a paint-covered marble from a spoon onto a piece of paper created a paint spot that marked where the marble hit the paper. When we asked, "How can we tell where Karli first dropped the painted golf ball?," Aisha responded, "There's a splash there!" Teon said, "Mine made the most big splash." We recorded the children's language and descriptions.

We built on the children's interest in splash marks by asking, "How could you make different kinds of splashes?" We dropped different-size balls and other objects. The children then varied the height from which they dropped objects, first by standing on a chair, then from the climber outside. When the chil-

dren suggested throwing things, we hung a sheet against a wall and they experimented. These experiences addressed standards related to scientific inquiry, problem solving, motor skills, and curiosity.

The children tried several balls at once in their paintings and used their senses to observe the results. Once again, they were developing basic science skills. They talked about the different sounds the balls made as they hit the surface, like *sploosh* and *bonk*. They began to understand that changing the direction of a force (tipping the box up) had two outcomes. It changed the direction of the balls, and it affected how fast the balls rolled. These are two key concepts in physical science. They also understood that balls with different textures produced different results. They commented, "Look at all the dots" about a Wiffle ball, and "It makes bigger lines" about a tennis ball.

We moved marble rolling outside where a big piece

of paper on a large paved area served as the paint surface. Outdoors, the activities required teamwork. As one group made a giant painting with plastic-covered playground balls, the wind began blowing. The entire group cooperated to move the balls across the area and keep the paper from blowing away. When they finished the painting, the teachers and children worked together to get it safely inside.

Conclusion

Our original goal was to use marble painting to help children understand and apply the skills of scientific inquiry. We hoped the activities would help them develop an understanding of motion. Our documentation—including photographs, videotapes, and observation notes—showed that after the marble painting activities, most of the children had begun to understand these skills and concepts.

However, we soon noticed that the "simple" science activity had become complex. Marble painting addressed many benchmarks, including some related to language arts, physical development, approaches to learning, and social and emotional development. The children actively engaged in developmentally appropriate experiences that were richly satisfying and meaningful to them. The classroom teachers, through thoughtful preparation, questioning, and detailed observation, had enriched a simple science activity.

Ideas for Using Open-Ended Questions

- Think of open-ended questions that support learning when planning activities. Write the questions on an index card.
- Keep the index cards handy so all teachers can use them to ask questions when children participate in the activity.
- Plan open-ended questions related to classroom learning centers. Write the questions on index cards and post them in the centers. Use these reminders to ask children questions about their play.
- Take index cards to the playground. Observe children's play outside and ask open-ended questions if appropriate.

REFERENCE

NAEYC & NAECS/SDE (National Association of Early Childhood Specialists in State Departments of Education). 2002. "Early Learning Standards: Creating the Conditions for Success." Joint position statement. Washington, DC: NAEYC. www.naeyc.org/files/naeyc/file/positions/position_statement.pdf.

Creatures in Your Gardening Curriculum

Alyse C. Hachey and Deanna Bulter

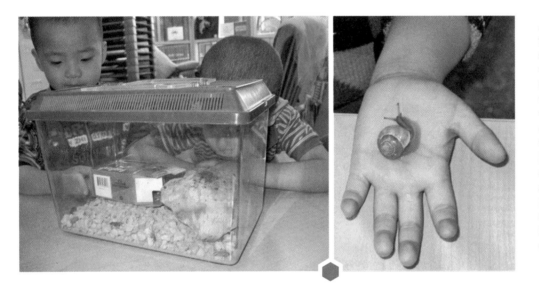

After the children planted their spring seeds, Nina said sadly, "Now we have to wait." To keep the children interested in gardening, we explored related topics while we waited. The children had had little exposure to nature, and some already had negative attitudes about tiny critters. I hoped an exploration of small animals that live in the garden might spark their scientific interest in, and appreciation of, these natural wonders.

Insects and other creatures are crucial to gardening. They aerate the soil, deposit nutrients, and eat other animals that harm plants. Because of their creepy reputation, they are often overlooked in the classroom. Yet firsthand experiences observing and handling small creatures can help preschoolers develop a healthy, curious attitude toward them, rather than one of fear or disgust. Watching yellow jackets sip apple cider is much more educational than shooing them away. Learning that bees pollinate plants so that fruit is produced shows children the importance of bees in their lives.

Bringing insects and other small creatures into the classroom allows children to observe stages of development in their life cycle. It is amazing to watch a caterpillar spinning a cocoon and emerging later as a butterfly! Through such experiences children can take on the role of biologists at their level of cognitive development.

Connecting Creatures With Science

A gardening curriculum that includes investigation of small animals encourages scientific attitudes, process skills, and content knowledge.

Scientific attitudes. In order for children to develop a strong curiosity about nature and the natural world, we must foster their innate curiosity with hands-on experiences. Caring for insects and small garden animals in the classroom helps children understand, appreciate, and gain enthusiasm for these creatures. They can also build a sense of responsibility and respect for living things.

Scientific process skills. Exposure to and interaction with small garden creatures promotes focused observation and data collection. Children can use the data to compare, contrast, and classify. They can chart and graph the eating and growth patterns of their creatures.

Scientific content knowledge. Through caring for and observing insects and small garden animals, children can begin to understand what distinguishes living from nonliving things. They learn what the necessities for survival are and animal characteristics and behavior.

Exploring these creatures addresses National Science Education Standards (National Research Council

1996) by allowing children to learn about life cycles, characteristics of common organisms, and how animals and the environment work as a system.

Mini-Beast Basics

Go local. Study garden animals common to your area. This way, classroom observations can carry over to what the children see in the play yard and their communities. Talk with local gardeners or conduct an Internet search of "[insert your state] local invertebrates" to find small native animals. Community gardeners, whether professional or not, are usually enthusiastic and willing to invite classes to their gardens and share their nature experiences. Also seek out nearby botanical gardens.

Ants may be the first garden creatures that come to mind. Although ants are interesting to study, keep those explorations on the playground or use a sealed ant habitat. Because of their size, ants don't offer the best hands-on exploration, and they can easily get loose! Crickets, ladybugs, mealworms, snails, earthworms, and caterpillars offer better scientific exploration. They are relatively easy to care for and available cheaply at many pet stores or in the backyard.

Take care. Provide what the small animals need to thrive—food, water, and any environmental specifics. Three useful websites for insect and small animal care are www.petbugs.com, www.earthlife.net/insects /carelist.html, and www.amentsoc.org/insects/ caresheets. Plan for what happens to the animals at the end of the school year. (For example, before releasing the classroom crickets in a park, learn whether introducing nonnative insects will upset the balance of nature there.)

Vivariums are indoor enclosures that simulate the natural environments of small animals. Many garden animals can live in vivariums made from common household materials. Snails can thrive in a clear plastic bucket or glass jar when the container has air holes on the lid and is filled with damp soil and decaying debris, such as twigs, dead leaves, and fruit rinds. Similarly, crickets do well in a clear, aerated bucket or jar filled with sand, twigs, pebbles, and grass. Crickets love to

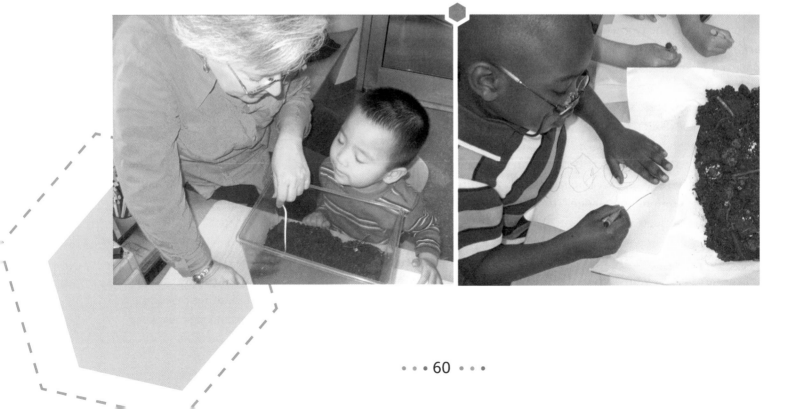

hide, so challenge the children to create hiding places. Do a search of "[your animal of interest] habitat" at www.ehow.com or see the resources on page 62 for more ideas on creating safe homes for garden animals.

Don't BUG me. The term *bug* is often used to name any unidentified garden insect; however, it is correctly used for only Heteroptera (also called true bugs). True bugs include bedbugs, stinkbugs, water striders, and several others. Lightning bugs and ladybugs are insects—not bugs. They are actually beetles. Spiders are arachnids, not bugs or insects.

Being scientifically correct is important, but using the name *bugs* is extremely common; try not to criticize children or parents who use the term. Many books incorrectly use bugs and *insects* interchangeably (even some listed in this article!). In the classroom, rather than incorrectly referring to unidentified animals, use the terms *small animals, small creatures*, or *mini-beasts*. To expand children's vocabulary, use the specific name of the creature whenever possible. Avoid negative labels, such as creepy crawlies.

Use the distinction between bugs and insects as an opportunity to explore with the children. *Bugs Are Insects*, by Anne Rockwell, is a terrific nonfiction picture book full of colorful collages. It introduces basic concepts for differentiating insects, bugs, spiders, and other kinds of small creatures.

Think inclusively. Because insects and small animals are so different from us, people develop strong attitudes about them—either as amazing or creepy. If you are not ready for real creatures in the classroom, you can add them through nonfiction and picture books,

posters, and models. Add plastic insects, high-quality soil, and small garden tools to the sensory table to acknowledge the role of insects in the garden.

Encourage children to investigate small creatures on the playground by putting out a dish of sugar water and offering magnifying glasses. Children can explore and develop questions about insects that foster their curiosity and diminish fear. Even checking your response to a spider in the classroom can make a difference. Instead of "Ew, kill it!" respond with "What is it doing? What do you notice about it? Let's take it out where it belongs." When you make this simple choice, you may affect children's lifelong attitudes—and their later interest in this important part of our natural world.

I brought snails into the classroom. The children were fascinated by their slow movement, long tentacles with eyes on them, and the shiny trail they left as they moved across paper. Adding food coloring to the paper, we observed our snails "painting"— what an amazing way to explore animal movement! We looked at models of insects and added them to the soil in our sensory table. We read stories and discussed the differences among insects, spiders, and other small animals. The children studied earthworms that lived in a container of soil, and crickets and snails housed in separate vivariums, and compost critters. One day, Aliyah said, "I'm not afraid of bugs anymore." "YES!" I thought to myself. It was such a rewarding moment. I had accomplished an important goal—helping children become interested in, and not afraid of, small garden creatures.

Books for Children

The Best Book of Bugs (2005), by Claire Llewellyn. Eye-catching illustrations and basic facts on common insects and other creatures such as spiders, snails, and worms.

Big Book of Bugs (2000), by Theresa Greenaway. Colorful, large-size photographs of insects, plus interesting facts and figures.

Bugs! (2000), by Patricia McKissack and Frederick McKissack, illus. by Mike Cressy. A guide to insects for young children, with colorful action pictures.

Bugs Are Insects (2001), by Anne Rockwell, illus. by Steve Jenkins. A preschool-level book with easy-to-read information introducing common insects and explaining differences between insects and spiders.

Insect (2007), by Laurence Mound. Though written for 8-year-olds and up, young children and adults can enjoy reading and looking at the large pictures and diagrams together.

Insects in Action (Level 1) (2012), by Thea Feldman and the American Museum of Natural History. A preschool-level book about the big things small creatures can do.

Websites

The Adventures of Herman the Worm. Fun facts about worms, including games and activities. http://urbanext.illinois.edu/worms.

Bug Art. Activities and ideas for insect-related drama activities and art. http://museumvictoria.com.au/pages/2085/bugs-bugs-bugs-drama-art.pdf.

Child Care Lounge. Insect-related songs, art, and recipes. www.childcarelounge.com/Caregivers/bug.htm.

Early Years Experience. A listing of mini-beast picture books that appeal to young children. www.bigeyedowl.co.uk/show_books.php?t=14.

Entomology for Beginners. Straightforward facts and explanations about various insects. www.bijlmakers.com/entomology/begin.htm.

Insect World. An interactive site that lets children play educational games about insects in various environments. www.britishcouncil.org/kids-games-insect-world.htm.

National Insect Week. Lists nonfiction picture and early reader books, along with interesting websites, poetry, music, and journals about insects. http://nationalinsectweek.co.uk/education_resources.htm.

Books for Teachers

Creepy Crawlies and the Scientific Method: More Than 100 Hands-On Science Experiments for Children (1993), by Sally Kneidel. Everything you need to know to keep and explore a variety of small animals.

Insectigations: 40 Hands-On Activities to Explore the Insect World (2005), by Cindy Blobaum. Information and activities for 7- to 10-year-olds that can be adapted for younger ages.

Snail Trails and Tadpole Tails: Nature Education for Young Children (1993), by Richard Cohen and Betty Phillips Tunick. Shares the stories of two teachers who created mini-habitats in their preschool classrooms. It contains detailed how-to information and resources.

Supporting Dual Language Learners

Exploring the lives of garden creatures will include some sophisticated vocabulary. Typically, dual language learners need extra time to practice and build their understanding of these experiences. Make sure they have plenty of opportunities to use the same words at other times and in other contexts. Use pictures and the new words to make puzzles or craft projects, incorporate the words into songs and stories with accompanying movements, and create books or PowerPoint displays that the children can go back to as often as needed to learn the new words and concepts.

REFERENCE

National Research Council. 1996. *National Science Education Standards*. Washington, DC: The National Academies Press. www.nap.edu/catalog.php?record_id=4962.

Discovering Science Learning Center

Laura J. Colker

Life Science

- Observe plants and animals.
- Predict what will happen if plants don't get enough water or light.
- Compare living and nonliving things.

Physical Science

- Observe light and shadows.
- Study the properties of magnets.
- Explore movement, weight, and speed with pulleys and ramps.

Earth and Environmental Science

- See how natural objects are alike and different (stones and shells).
- Observe and record the weather.
- Recycle to protect the environment.

Math

- Weigh materials.
- Collect, count, and sort objects.
- Gather, organize, and present data (What items can a magnet pick up?).

Language and Literacy

- Make and post signs, such as Guppy Feeding at 3:00 p.m.
- Document experiments in journals.
- Learn vocabulary: *experiment, predict, cocoon, X-ray, pulley, ramp.*

- Locate the discovery center near natural light.
- Use the windowsill for growing plants and displaying prisms.
- Use trays to hold discovery materials such as Ping-Pong balls and straws or magnets with magnetic marbles.
- Incorporate materials related to all kinds of science, including *physical science*, *life science*, and *earth and environmental science*.
- Look for materials that preschoolers see in their daily lives, for example stones, shells, and mechanical objects—like clocks—that children can take apart.

- Remember, science materials are every-where. Look for seeds, flowers, leaves, pine-cones, stones, shells, insects, birds' nests. Use sunlight and shadows.
- Ask doctors, dentists, and veterinarians to donate old X-rays of bones or teeth.
- Use two plastic bottles, water, and duct tape to simulate tornados. Combine baking soda, vinegar, and dishwashing soap to simulate volcanic eruptions. Search "tornado in a bottle" for directions.

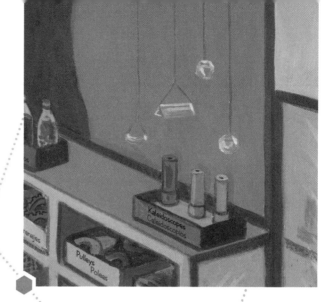

Beyond the Basics

- While working on projects or themes, add related items to the center. If studying ponds, bring in lily pads to examine.
- Add a light table to expand a study of light using prisms, mirrors, and kaleidoscopes. (See article on light tables in *Teaching Young Children*, vol. 2, no. 4.)
- Conduct experiments in the sand and water tables: Predict which items will sink or float. Discover how sand changes when you add water.
- Extend discovery to the outdoors. Plant a garden. Feed the birds. Blow bubbles. Measure shadows. Collect rain.
- Offer sensory experiences in empty sand or water tubs—fill with packing peanuts, grass, snow, ice cubes, or Oobleck.
- Connect science with art. Children can draw patterns they notice in nature or use natural materials to create collages.

Include Children's Families and Cultures

- Ask families to contribute old or broken items that children can take apart and put together. Make sure items are safe before including in the center.
- Encourage families to take their children on nature walks or to join the class on one of its walks.
- Share documentation of children's experiments on bulletin boards, in email newsletters, and on the program website.
- Provide instructions and materials for experiments families and children can do at home.
- Ask families for science ideas to explore in the center.

A Place for Studying Our Bodies

Laura J. Colker

A place for studying our bodies, housed in the discovering science learning center, offers children tools and space to examine and learn about the human body, inside and out. Children can build inquiry skills as they observe, compare and contrast, form hypotheses, conduct experiments, and report findings in graphs and charts.

Materials—In addition to items shown here, you can rotate in exciting learning tools, including

- Books such as *First Encyclopedia of the Human Body* (Fiona Chandler); *Inside Your Outside: All About the Human Body* (Tish Rabe)
- A three-dimensional human body puzzle
- Charts about body parts
- Posters of the digestive, nervous, circulatory, and skeletal systems

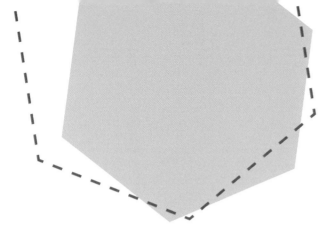

What Children Do and Learn

Math

- Show awareness of positions in space when they place body parts on a cutout of the human body.
- Measure and compare the lengths of bones on the skeleton, using a tape measure or yarn.
- Make charts and graphs about body parts and taking care of ourselves.

Language and Literacy

- Enjoy and value reading and explore features of nonfiction texts when they look at books about bodies.
- Demonstrate knowledge of print and vocabulary development when they tell a story about the human body using the word wall entries.
- Understand that words and pictures go together when they return materials to appropriate places on labeled shelves.

Art and Music

- Sing and act out songs such as "Head, Shoulders, Knees, and Toes."
- Make life-size replicas of their bodies out of papier-mâché and paint them. Make plaster molds of hands and feet.

Companion Studies

- **Studying body unmentionables (hiccups and burps and gas—oh my!):** Children can do experiments to learn how acids in the stomach make gas, how chemical interactions cause mucus, and how the chemicals in saliva break down starches.
- **Looking at fingerprints:** Children can learn how to collect and study fingerprints. They will need oil for coating fingers, a glass to hold and leave behind fingerprints, cocoa powder for dusting prints, a soft brush for brushing off cocoa powder residue, transparent tape to lift prints, and blank index cards for displaying prints.

Setup Tips

- Locate where there is wall space for hanging charts and graphs or space for chart stands.
- Place shelving under and on top of a table to save space.
- Use a window as a source of light for viewing X-rays.
- Make sure the posters and images displayed in the center depict different genders, races, and cultures.
- Include materials to represent each of the body's six systems—the *circulatory system*, the *nervous system*, the *skeletal system*, the *digestive system*, the *respiratory system*, and the *muscular system*.

Include Children's Families and Cultures

- Ask families to help translate words on signs and charts into home languages.
- Invite families to send in photos that children can use to make collages about body parts.
- Encourage families to contribute to the class planning web about studying the human body.
- Invite families to come in and participate with activities in the center. They may want to participate in crafts, help with puzzles, or play games.
- Ask families to share how they take care of their bodies.

Budget Stretchers

- Ask health providers to donate out-of-date X-rays, stethoscopes, and other safe-to-use medical items for use in the center.
- Look for magnifying glasses, mirrors, and digital cameras or microscopes at yard sales and thrift shops, on Craigslist, and through Freecycle (www.freecycle.org).
- Make puzzles, lotto games, and games like Pin-the-Body-Part-on-the-Torso. Provide materials and instructions so families can volunteer to help make these items, or plan a family workshop for making these items and others.

Exploring Trees

Ellen Hall, Desarie Kennedy, Alison Maher, and Lisa Stevens

Boulder Journey School, a private school in Boulder, Colorado, where we teach, welcomes more than 200 children from 6 weeks to 6 years of age and their families. Our study of the schools for young children in Reggio Emilia, Italy, led us to re-examine how we organize our curriculum. We now support long-term classroom investigations that last several days, weeks, months, and even years. Children can research a topic, concept, or question in depth. Projects focus on meaningful, relevant learning experiences through which children and adults build knowledge together.

Locals boast that Boulder has more than 300 days of sunshine a year; thus some of our long-term investigations are sparked by the children's interactions with the natural world. At the beginning of the school year, we observed and documented the children's play and listened to their conversations, comments, theories, and questions about trees. Their curiosity about the trees outside their classroom launched a yearlong investigation of trees in one of our 4- and 5-year-olds classrooms.

The children drew many pictures of trees. We challenged them to slow down and focus on the details—roots, branches, and leaves.

We offered paint and clay, provided cameras and opportunities to take photographs of the trees, and encouraged children's explorations using the languages of music, movement, dance, and drama.

Each experience added to the children's collective knowledge of trees. The children's conversations told us that they were making connections between their own lives and the lives of the trees.

"Leaves are the blankets to keep the trees warm."
—4-year-old child

"Roots of all the trees in the world meet in the center of the Earth to drink water together." —5-year-old child

Every child had a story to tell about a special tree in his or her life. One 5-year-old girl began sculpting clay trees. She was inspired by her relationship with a tree in her neighborhood park. She said that this tree was made for children:

"There is this park down the street from me, and you just have to walk down the sidewalk, and on the grass, there is this tree, and on the tree there is a bump. It's for kids to step on it, and I can step on it, and they just climb on it. It kind of has lots of branches, and sometimes I go high. It has these little roots sticking out of the ground. We just step on them, so we can swing on the branches."

She invited us to meet her tree, so we organized a group excursion to her neighborhood park. The children climbed the trunk almost as if it were a rite of passage or an entrance into another world. They discovered how the tree made them feel—joyful, brave, strong, safe.

Back in the classroom, another child formed a clay tree and said, "I want my tree to do ballet." This led to the exploration of the relationship between the children's tree representations and body movements.

In January, midway through the project, we paused

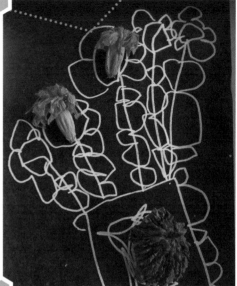

to reflect on our work. The children and adults had experienced and learned a lot about trees. The children said they wanted to make their work public.

They worked together and shared their individual expertise while planning, producing, and performing a show, "The Lonely Tree." Sculptures, drawings, and stories inspired costumes, scenery design, choreography, and song lyrics.

Although this group of children has graduated and entered kindergarten, we know that the memory of this work will influence their approach to future experiences.

Books About Underwater Life

Lauren Baker

Young children are just beginning to learn about animal habitats. While they may see many animals during their daily lives, like birds and insects, they may know less about animals that live in the water. These books will introduce different types of underwater life.

Coral Reefs, by Gail Gibbons. 2007. Holiday House.

Coral reefs are a bright, exciting environment that is new to many preschoolers. This book uses detailed drawings and labels to bring the habitat to life. The colorful illustrations will fascinate young children; teachers can share details from the informational text about where reefs are found and what kinds of animals make coral their home.

Hooray for Fish! by Lucy Cousins. 2005. Candlewick Press.

Lucy Cousins, author of the famous Maisy series, has written a book introducing fish to children. As a little fish swims around the ocean, she greets all the different kinds of fish she sees, some fanciful. This sweet book with rhyming text is a fun read for a preschool class.

Mister Seahorse, by Eric Carle. 2004. Philomel Books.

Mr. Seahorse floats around near the ocean floor, passing his fellow sea creatures. Many of the animals he passes are hidden in ocean vegetation. Children can look for them in Carle's intricate collage habitats.

Jump, Frog, Jump! by Robert Kalan,
illus. by Byron Barton. 1989. Greenwillow
Books.

Jump, Frog, Jump! offers children a
look at life in and near a pond. The story
follows the sequence of events that occur
after a frog jumps into the pond. As he
jumps after a fly that crosses his path, we
see a hungry fish, snake, and turtle chas-
ing after their own lunches. The frequent
repetition in the text allows preschoolers
to be involved in the storytelling.

After Reading These Books

Build a fish. At group time, talk to the children about what
they noticed about the fish in these books. "What do fish
look like?" "Where do they live?" In small groups, have children build their own fish from a variety of materials. Include
different items, from construction paper to clothing scraps,
to use as scales and fins. Later, have the children create a
place for the fish to live, including sand, rocks, or different
kinds of mesh to represent coral.

Compare lengths. Cut string to the lengths of different
underwater animals. Include very small creatures, like a
tadpole, and very large ones, like a dolphin, shark, or whale.
Have the children pair off. Each will hold one end of a string
and pull it tight so they can see how large the animals are.
For a challenge, have the children organize animals, small-
est to largest. Then compare the lengths of the animals to
the heights of the children.

Make a water habitat. Turn the water table into an ocean,
pond, or river. Include plastic fish, sea stars, frogs, and
other underwater animals. Add the types of vegetation that
you might find in a body of water in your area—plastic lily
pads, cattails, or seaweed.

Worms to Beans

Jean Thompson Bird

In the fall and winter, the children in our preschool program raise worms in the classroom and use the worms to compost food scraps. In the spring, we use the worm castings (manure) to fertilize the soil in our garden. The children plant the seeds, transplant the seedlings in the garden, then watch them grow until the vegetables are ready to pick and eat.

Children respond enthusiastically to caring for the worms and plants, and enjoy tasting food they grow. Families are inspired by the project and begin composting, gardening, and establishing their own worm farms.

Teachers can continue the farm and garden from year to year. Worms will continue to reproduce as long as they are fed every few weeks and get new bedding every few months.

Why do this activity? Children gain respect for living things and their contributions to the earth.

What can children learn? Worm life cycles, recycling, composting, conservation, and plant growth, as well as nutrition concepts.

Vocabulary words: *compost, recycling, conservation, castings, fertilizer, roots, stems, leaves, flowers, fruits, seeds, seedlings, stretch and squeeze, aerate, shovel, rake, hoe, primary and secondary leaves*

Materials:

Worm farms

- Worm composting bin (17" x 13" x 11")
- Worms (collect 20–40 earthworms or purchase 1 lb. of much smaller red worms by mail)
- Bucket (1 gallon)
- Garden soil (6 cups)
- Newspaper (shredded to fill a ½ gallon container)
- Water
- Hand rake
- Food processor
- Fruit and vegetable food scraps
- Large plastic sheet or tablecloth
- Plastic airtight containers of any size

Vegetable garden

- Potting soil
- Egg cartons or small recycled food containers
- Seeds (sugar snap pea and green bean or other vegetables grown in your area)
- Low fencing to enclose the garden
- Topsoil
- Tools (child-size rakes, shovels, hoes)

Prepare for the Activity

1. Purchase or gather the materials listed above.
2. Write to families to explain the steps in the project, what children will be learning, and invite them to be involved.

3. Introduce the project to the children. Explain what you will be doing throughout the year. Ask children what they know about worms and what questions they have. Record their responses on a concept web and post it in the classroom.

4. Add books about worms to the classroom library and read them to children.

Lead Small and Large Groups

Children and teachers work together to carry out the steps below. Involve one or more children at a time, depending on the task and children's interest in participating.

Worm farms

1. Make the worm bedding. Shred newspaper into one-inch squares. Mix a half gallon of this newspaper (loosely packed) with six cups of garden soil and enough water so the bedding is moist. It will look like solid, moist mud. Fill the bin with bedding until it is three-quarters full.

2. Add worms. Place the worms on top of the bedding. The worms will dig into the bedding in about two days.

3. Feed the worms. Have children save fruit and vegetable scraps from their meals. Every two weeks, grind six cups of scraps in a food processor or cut them into fine pieces (it's easier for the worms to eat smaller pieces of food). Bury the pulp in one corner of the bin, alternating corners each time.

4. Separate the castings. Once a month, spread a plastic tablecloth on the floor, then dump out the worm bin. Worms will move to the bottom, so children can gently lift the top layers of soil. Repeat until worms are separated from most of the castings. Store the castings in an airtight container so they do not get hard and dry.

5. Repeat steps 1 through 4. Each time, put the worms into new bedding. Continue the process throughout the year.

Vegetable garden

1. Prepare the garden beds. Three weeks before outdoor planting, turn the soil, remove rocks and sticks, mix in three-inches of top soil, and put up the garden fence.

2. Grow seedlings. Fill egg cartons with ¾ potting soil and ¼ castings. Plant seeds as directed on packets. In a few days, the seeds will sprout and leaves appear. When the second set of leaves appear, it is time to transplant the seedlings in the garden bed.

3. Plant seedlings in the prepared garden. Follow seed packet instructions.
4. Care for the plants. Every few weeks, add a handful of castings around each plant and gently mix into soil. Weed and water frequently.
5. Harvest the crop. When the vegetables are ripe, pick, rinse, eat, and enjoy! Talk about why vegetables help us stay healthy.

Respond to Individual Needs

1. If some children are hesitant to touch worms, invite them to observe with magnifying glasses so they can see them without having to touch them. Over time, most children get used to holding the worms.
2. Help children with disabilities participate in the project. Provide one-on-one support, have them work with a partner, and offer hand-over-hand guidance as appropriate.
3. Make a list of key words in English and children's home languages. Place the list near the children's books on worms and gardens.

Follow Up After the Activity

1. Have children document the project. They can draw, take photos, and write or dictate captions to create a timeline or book. They can measure, record data, and create graphs.
2. Use the documentation to review the project steps and reinforce learning.

Involve Families

1. Make a worm bin that interested children and families can borrow or keep. We use a small opaque plastic container with holes in the lid. Take some worms from the class worm farm to start family worm farms.
2. Invite families to help water and weed the class garden. Suggest they start a garden of their own.
3. Provide project updates in a family newsletter or on a bulletin board.

Children's Books About Worms

Wiggling Worms at Work (2004), by Wendy Pfeffer, illus. by Steve Jenkins

Yucky Worms (2009), by Vivian French, illus. by Jessica Ahlberg

The Worm (2014), by Elise Gravel

Let's Find Out! Preschoolers as Scientific Explorers

Kimberly Brenneman

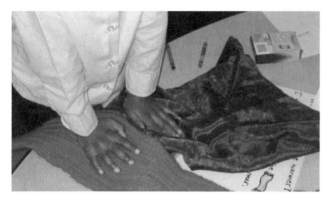

"Cold water! Cold water!"

"Put 'em on your hands. Then put 'em in the water."

"Which one is freezing? That one or that one?"

I t was winter in the northeast United States, so a scientific exploration of the ways that people and animals stay warm in cold environments was of great interest to the preschoolers in this class. During large group time one day, the children and teachers discussed ways humans protect themselves from the cold. The children knew a lot about this topic, so it made a good starting point for exploring related ideas. Then the teacher asked, "How do animals stay warm when it is very cold outside?" The children knew less about this, so the teacher helped them research the question. Then she introduced a science activity to let the children find the answer to the question themselves.

Why do this activity? Scientific explorers, both tall and small, ask questions about objects, living things, and events that interest or puzzle them. Young children are often described as natural scientists. They earn this description because they engage in many of the same behaviors scientists do.

What can children learn? Science is not just a list of facts that other people have discovered. It's a process that anyone can participate in and contribute to. Firsthand investigations and experiences make learning more meaningful to children. Engaging in scientific investigation supports children's language, math, science, and reasoning skills. Applying the scientific method is useful for all kinds of problem solving. As children's learning partners, teachers can plan experiences that allow children to share their clever ideas and inspire them to keep exploring their world in scientific ways.

Vocabulary words: *Blubber, insulate, experiment, trial, test, predict, hypothesis, conclusion*

Materials:

- Zipper-top plastic bags
- Vegetable shortening
- A spoon
- A small ice chest
- Ice water

Prepare for the Activity

1. Make a blubber glove. Teachers fill one zipper-top plastic bag with vegetable shortening. Then they turn another bag inside out, place it inside the first bag, and press the closures together to seal the blubber inside. Use duct tape to reinforce the closures.
2. Make an unfilled glove. Children turn an empty bag inside out, place it inside another empty bag, and press the closures together.

Lead Small Groups

1. Invite four to six children to participate.
2. Introduce the blubber glove, the unfilled glove, and the new vocabulary.
3. Children take turns wearing both gloves and putting their gloved hands into the cold water. (Remind children to keep the top parts of the gloves above the water level.)
4. Record the findings. Provide paper, pencils, and clipboards so children can draw or write about their observations. Children can write tallies or names on a chart to indicate their findings. Comparing the two gloves makes the investigation a true science exper-

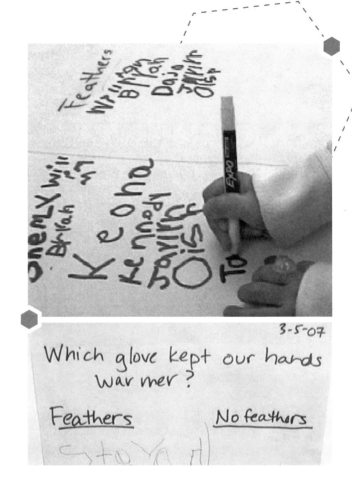

iment. Because the gloves are the same except for the blubber, children will know that it is the blubber (the vegetable shortening), and not some other difference, that insulates their hands from the cold of the ice water.

Respond to Individual Needs

Ask questions to get children thinking about this science activity. "Which glove do you think will keep your hand warmer?" "Which hand feels cold?" "Which hand feels warm?" "What pattern do you notice on the record chart?" "What do you think would happen if we put feathers in the glove?"

Follow Up After the Activity

Try using a different material, such as feathers or fabric, inside a glove. Then repeat the experience.

Involve Families

1. Announce the activity in a family newsletter or on a bulletin board.
2. Explain how families can use the scientific method to answer questions at home.
3. Invite families to volunteer in the classroom to help the children participate in this activity.

The Scientific Method

1. Question
2. Research
3. Predict
4. Investigate
5. Analyze
6. Communicate

Books

No Two Alike (2011), by Keith Baker

The Story of Snow: The Science of Winter's Wonder (2009), by Mark Cassino, With Jon Nelson

The First Day of Winter (2005), by Denise Fleming

Over and Under the Snow (2011), by Kate Messner, illus. by Christopher Silas Neal

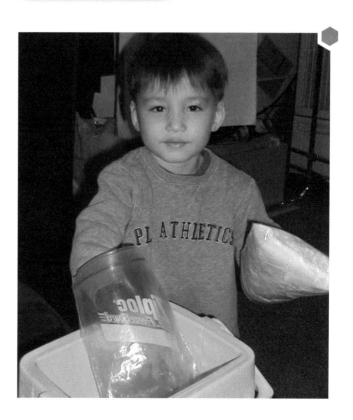

Ramps and Pathways: Physical Science for Preschoolers

Betty Zan and Rosemary Geiken

Ramps and pathways activities invite all children to use simple materials to gain science inquiry skills, learn science concepts, and have great fun in the process. We hope that the photos and text in this article will inspire teachers to learn more about the possibilities found in these simple materials.

Setting Up the Classroom

At first, introduce wood cove molding and marbles to the block center. Later, add variations, while keeping the basic ingredients unchanged.

Materials

Wood cove molding (also called coving). This molding is found in most hardware stores. Use coving that is 1¾ inches wide (marbles wobble too much on wider widths). Provide 18 sections of 1-, 2-, 3-, and

4-foot lengths (in small classrooms omit the 4-foot lengths).

Marbles and more. Include a variety of sizes so children can compare the movement of large and small marbles. Add variations such as steel marbles, blocks or other objects that do not roll, and items that roll differently (such as spools, egg-shaped objects, spheres with bumps).

Blocks. Offer wood unit blocks, large hollow wood blocks, large interlocking blocks, and large cardboard blocks.

Other supports. Provide large sponges, cardboard boxes (cut openings in them), plus shelves, chairs, tables, or other furniture.

Space

The best place for ramps is in the block center. Once children start building ramps, they want to build them bigger and bigger! But preschoolers can be very creative in small spaces. You might be able to use hallways, lunchrooms, and open conference rooms, or take the ramps outdoors.

Time

Children need plenty of time, every day and throughout the year, to explore the ramp materials. They might revisit the ideas they used the day before, reflect on what they did, and revise their thinking.

Exploring Big Ideas

1. Examine the ramps and pathways materials first, so you can understand the possibilities for learning.

    To be able to support young children's development of scientific knowledge and reasoning, teachers must understand how inclined planes work. Experiment and figure out (among other things) how to move a marble without touching it and how to make a marble go up a ramp section or turn a corner.

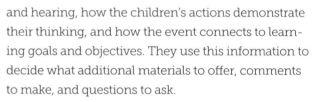

2. Create a learning environment that inspires and allows children to try out their interests and ideas.

When young children approach the ramp materials they try to figure out what they can do with them. They have ideas, and try out their ideas to see what will happen. They need to feel safe trying their ideas, without fear of failure. Instead of correcting children or giving them right answers, ask questions or make comments that inspire children's further experimentation.

3. Observe children closely to understand and assess their reasoning.

Effective observers know what they are seeing

and hearing, how the children's actions demonstrate their thinking, and how the event connects to learning goals and objectives. They use this information to decide what additional materials to offer, comments to make, and questions to ask.

A preschool teacher, who says she was "scared" to teach science, boasts that now "we are actually doing science every day and have a science center going daily."

4. Focus on children's reasoning rather than right answers.

Young children's investigations often lead to common erroneous ideas, or what science educators call preconceptions. For example, even after seeing a marble roll down an elevated incline and fly off the end, many children will still predict that a marble will drop straight down into a container when it reaches the end of a ramp. To help children correct their preconceptions, encourage continued experimentation.

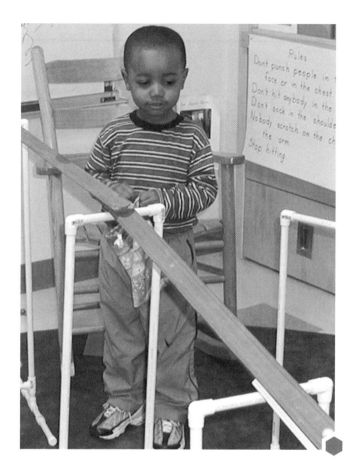

6. Integrate ramp activities with other curriculum areas.

Mathematics is everywhere: children use spatial reasoning to decide where to position blocks or how to align ramp sections; they experiment to figure out how to use angles so marbles will turn corners; they count blocks to compare heights and predict how many more blocks they will need. Ramp makers can create class books. For social studies, discuss the use of ramps in the workplace or by persons with disabilities. Children's ramp structures integrate art and architecture too.

Another preschool teacher says, "I do a lot more thinking about science and spend more time on science in the room with the children. I have science on the brain."

For more information on using ramps and pathways in your classroom, see NAEYC's book *Ramps & Pathways: A Constructivist Approach to Physics With Young Children*, by Rheta Devries and Christina Sales, or visit www.rampsandpathways.org.

5. Encourage children to share their experiences and results.

Have children work in groups and share ideas. Provide materials so children can draw and write about their ramp structures. Take photos of children's ramp structures and use them to prompt writing, drawing, and discussions. During group time, invite children to reflect on what they have done in the ramps center.

Ready, Set, Learn!
We're Off to the Moon

Marie Faust Evitt

It was the start of a new school day and yet another round of *Star Wars* play among a group of 4- and 5-year-olds in my preschool class. Some children brandished their invisible lightsabers and others ran from them. Every day they played basically the same game, showing little interest in art experiences, science explorations, or math games.

Tim, the assistant teacher, and I wanted to expand this *Star Wars* enthusiasm into more creative play and learning opportunities. During our brainstorm session, Tim suggested that we start a mission to the moon. The children could be astronauts and learn about space travel and the moon. I was enthusiastic about the possibilities for problem solving and building a rich curriculum based on this idea.

Introducing the Moon

We gathered useful information from a trip to the library and NASA's website, www.nasa.gov. Thinking that we could use cardboard boxes for building spaceships, I asked families for cereal boxes and local grocery stores for paper bags and big cardboard boxes.

At circle time a few days later, I dimmed the lights to make it like nighttime. I told the class, "Teacher Tim and I know many people love the *Star Wars* movies. Those are pretend stories. Do you know that real people called astronauts went into outer space in real spaceships all the way to the real moon? I'm going to read you a story about traveling to the moon."

The children were fascinated by the story of the first moon landing, *One Giant Leap*, by Robert Burleigh. At the end of the story I said, "You have powerful imaginations. I think you could become astronauts and pretend you are traveling to the moon. What do you think you'd need to be an astronaut?"

The children nearly launched themselves off the floor, hands waving.

"We need rockets."

"Helmets."

"Food."

So began our mission to the moon.

Curriculum Connections

Launching into outer space became the focus of the entire curriculum for several weeks. It provided opportunities to connect science, math, literacy, language, art, and drama. We read books and discussed different parts of a space mission. The children made a giant spaceship from large cardboard boxes and pretended they were rocketing to the moon and beyond. Mission control consisted of old telephones, obsolete computer keyboards, headphones, and other equipment made from milk jug lids set up on a table. The children made jet packs from cereal boxes, space helmets from paper bags, and smaller spaceships from paper towel and wrapping paper tubes. The children *became* astronauts.

Best of all, the explorations appealed to all the children in the class, not just the *Star Wars* crowd. The sense of adventure in blasting into space inspired imagination and cooperation.

Some early childhood educators believe that outer space can be too abstract and remote for young children. However, we discovered many age-appropriate, hands-on explorations that helped the preschoolers learn about our nearest neighbor in space while satisfying their desire to be big and powerful.

Astronaut food. After reading books and information from the NASA website (www.spaceflight.nasa.gov/living/spacefood/index.html), the children wanted to try eating the same way astronauts do—without the pull of gravity to keep food on plates and drinks in cups. They measured and mixed Tang, a powdered orange drink that became popular when astronauts took it into space in 1965. They ate applesauce in a way similar to how astronaut John Glenn did in 1962. (See the box on p. 93 for directions.)

Astronaut jumping. Math came alive when the children measured how high they can jump on Earth and learned how high that would be on the moon. The moon has less pull from gravity than the earth because it is smaller. You can jump six times higher on the moon than on the earth. Although preschoolers may not fully understand gravity, they understand more and less and that the moon is different in many ways from the earth.

We made a simple high jump stand by placing two small, rectangular unit blocks a yard apart and laying a yardstick across them. The children took turns jumping over this first height. If they knocked the yardstick off the blocks, they helped put it back and went to the end of the line for another turn. In the next round, the children decided if they wanted to raise the bar by adding a block to each side or if they wanted to keep it at the same height as before. They used a second yardstick to measure how high they jumped in inches. Then we stacked several unit blocks to show how high a moon jump would be. A jump four blocks high became a

Literature and Dramatic Play

During circle time Tim and I read aloud books that inspired discussions about what children would need to get to the moon. We acted out the dramatic story "An Adventure in Space," by musicians Greg and Steve. The children brainstormed the different adventures they might have. "We might see aliens." "We might run out of gas." "We might crash."

Later, sitting in their spaceship and at mission control, the children tried out their ideas.

"Check the controls."

"3-2-1 . . . Blast off!"

"Emergency. Emergency. We're going to crash."

"Turn the wheel!"

stack of 24 blocks. The children loved counting 24 blocks!

Crater explorations. We showed children photos of the Moon's surface. We introduced the word *crater*, a bowl-shaped hole created when a chunk of rock from space crashes into a moon or planet. We invited the children to explore how craters are created using pretend moondust. (See the box on p. 93 for recipe. Damp sand also works.) We provided several balls of varying weights and sizes (marbles, Ping-Pong, golf, tennis, baseball, and foam) and various round lids (such as those from milk jugs and yogurt containers) for measuring by comparison.

I put more than four inches of moondust in a large tub and invited children to predict what would happen when they dropped a ball from shoulder height without throwing or pushing it down. Would the dust fly out? Would the size of the crater be as big as a yogurt lid or smaller? After they dropped the ball and observed the crater size, they smoothed the dust with a tongue depressor. We continued the exploration by dropping objects of different sizes and weights from different heights. Children drew pictures and dictated their observations about the relationship between the size and weight of the ball and the size and depth of the crater.

Art and Science

Astronaut drawing. To help children imagine how it would feel to work inside a small spaceship without gravity, we challenged them to work in unusual positions. We taped drawing paper to the underside of tables so children could draw pictures while lying on their backs on the floor.

Gravity painting. This exuberant (but messy) experience uses old socks filled with sand to make *space rocks.* The children dipped space rocks in a mix of tempera paint, starch, and liquid soap (this mixture extends the paint and makes it easier to wash out of clothes). Then they held them above a long sheet of paper. I emphasized that gravity would do the work. The children just let go of the socks to see what would happen. *Splat!*

Language Arts

Storytelling. Children who rarely came to the writing table loved drawing pictures of spaceships and dictating space adventure stories. I used the following story starters: "Where would you like to travel in space?" "What do you think it would be like to live on the moon?" "What would you see on a trip to the moon?" An adult wrote down the children's stories, and I read them aloud at story time.

Conclusion

We celebrated the conclusion of our moon mission by acting out the first moon walk. The children turned the sandbox into a model of the moon, complete with craters. They wore their jet packs and space helmets. They took turns walking on the moon, planting the American flag, and saying, "That's one small step for man, one giant leap for mankind."

We're ready for new adventures in learning. To infinity and beyond!

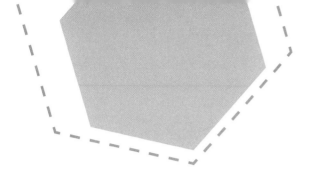

Eat Like an Astronaut

With a little bit of assistance, children can make and eat food like astronauts.

1. In a small, sealable plastic bag, measure and add 1 teaspoon orange powdered drink mix (Tang) and ½ cup water.
2. Seal the bag and gently squeeze it to mix the Tang and water.
3. Open a small space at the top, put a straw in that space, and drink through the straw.

Astronauts in space make as little garbage as possible. We reused the plastic bags to eat applesauce. After finishing the drink

1. Add two large spoonfuls of applesauce to the bag.
2. Seal the bag shut.
3. Snip off a bottom corner (with adult help, if needed).
4. Suck the applesauce through the hole.

Pretend Moondust

4 cups dried coffee grounds (Save your own or ask families or a coffee shop to save used grounds for you.)
4 cups cornstarch
2 cups sand

Measure ingredients and stir with spoons and hands.

I always emphasize that we are using our imagination when we make pretend moondust. This dust didn't really come from the moon. It looks and feels like it could be moondust.

Book Suggestions

What the Moon Is Like (2000), by Franklyn M. Branley, illus. by True Kelley

One Giant Leap (2009), by Robert Burleigh

If You Decide to Go to the Moon (2005), by Faith McNulty, illus. by Steven Kellogg

Living in Space (2004), by Patricia Whitehouse

Astronaut Handbook (2008), by Meghan McCarthy

Moonshot: The Flight of Apollo 11 (2009), by Brian Floca

Discovering Science Learning Center Checklist

Laura J. Colker

ou can complete this checklist for the discovering science learning center in your classroom on your own or with a teaching colleague. When you are finished, review the items you rated as "rarely" and create an action plan to help change the rating to "sometimes" or "regularly."

	Regularly	Sometimes	Rarely
1. Children choose to visit the discovering science center every day.	○	○	○
2. Children know and follow the rules for the discovering science center.	○	○	○
3. The center is located away from louder areas, such as the music and movement center.	○	○	○
4. Materials are stored in labeled containers and shelves within children's reach.	○	○	○
5. There are books about science and scientists.	○	○	○
6. Children can save their creations and complete them later.	○	○	○
7. Children have fun and express pleasure in experimenting in the discovering science center.	○	○	○
8. While playing in the discovering science center, children can express thoughts and feelings and build skills in all domains.	○	○	○
9. The discovering science center is stocked with			
• Various items for children to experiment with, such as magnets, prisms, and mirrors	○	○	○
• Natural materials for children to explore, such as seashells, small stones, seeds, and pinecones	○	○	○
• Paper and writing instruments that allow children to document their discoveries	○	○	○
• Books that relate to children's current scientific interests and inspire new interests	○	○	○
10. Teachers extend children's play by			
• Asking questions	○	○	○
• Offering ideas	○	○	○
• Commenting on their work	○	○	○
• Providing new materials that offer different experiences and challenges.	○	○	○

Credits

The following are selections published previously in *Teaching Young Children* and the issues in which they appeared:

Math

"Discovering Shapes and Space in Preschool," April 2014

"Math and Manipulatives Learning Center," December 2011

"A Place for Making Games and Puzzles," October 2012

"You Can Count on Math," October 2008

"Books About Counting to 10 and Higher," June 2013

"Using Children's Books to Introduce Math," February 2010

"Preschoolers Getting in Shape," June 2014

"Everyday Math Manipulatives," April 2010

"Sorting Activities for Preschoolers," June 2012

"Developing Math Games Based on Children's Books," December 2008

Science

"Exploring Motion," February 2013

"Creatures in Your Gardening Curriculum," June 2012

"Discovering Science Learning Center," April 2010

"A Place for Studying Our Bodies," December 2011

"Exploring Trees," October 2011

"Books About Underwater Life," April 2012

"Worms to Beans," April 2010

"Let's Find Out! Preschoolers as Scientific Explorers," October 2013

"Ramps and Pathways: Physical Science for Preschoolers," December 2010

"Ready, Set, Learn! We're Off to the Moon," February 2014

The following are adaptations of articles published previously in *Young Children* and the issues in which they appeared:

Math

"Happy 100th Birthday, Unit Blocks!" November 2013

"Developing Math Games Based on Children's Literature," January 2003

Science

"Early Learning Standards in Action: Young Children Exploring Motion," September 2006

"Creatures in the Classroom: Including Insects and Small Animals in Your Preschool Gardening Curriculum," March 2012

"Ramps and Pathways: Developmentally Appropriate, Intellectually Rigorous, and Fun Physical Science," January 2010

"Let's Find Out! Preschoolers as Scientific Explorers," November 2009

About the Authors

Lauren Baker is an assistant editor at NAEYC. She writes and edits for the magazine *Teaching Young Children*.

Jean Thompson Bird lives in Pittsburgh, Pennsylvania. She works at the Carnegie Mellon Children's School as an early childhood educator.

Mary Teresa Bowne, EdD, lives on an acreage near White, South Dakota. She works at South Dakota State University as an associate professor in early childhood education.

Kimberly Brenneman lives in Metuchen, New Jersey. She works at Rutgers University and directs the Early Childhood STEM Lab at the National Institute for Early Education Research.

Deanna L. Butler, MS, is a head teacher at the Borough of Manhattan Community College Early Childhood Center. She is an educator of 3- to 6-year-olds with 10 years of experience teaching in the boroughs of Brooklyn and Manhattan in New York City.

Douglas H. Clements, PhD, lives in Denver, Colorado. He works at the University of Denver as a professor, the Kennedy Endowed Chair in Early Childhood Learning, and the executive director of the Marsico Institute for Early Learning and Literacy.

Laura J. Colker, EdD, of Washington, DC, is president of L.J. Colker & Associates. In addition to being a contributing editor of *Teaching Young Children*, she has authored more than 100 publications and instructional guides, including co-authorship of *The Creative Curriculum for Preschool*.

Kay M. Cutler lives in White, South Dakota. She works at South Dakota State University as a professor in early childhood education.

Linda Dauksas, EdD, lives in Burr Ridge, Illinois. She is an associate professor and director of early childhood education at Elmhurst College. There she teaches courses in early childhood education, including assessment, environment, methods for early childhood special education, and working with families and communities.

Meghan Dombrink-Green received her master's degree from Johns Hopkins University and served as a Fulbright English Teaching Assistant to Cyprus. She is an associate editor at NAEYC, working primarily on *Teaching Young Children*.

Marie Faust Evitt lives in Mountain View, California. She is a lead teacher at the Mountain View Parent Nursery School. Her article is adapted from her book, *Thinking BIG, Learning BIG: Connecting Science, Math, Literacy, and Language in Early Childhood*.

Amy Freshwater, PhD, is an assistant professor of child development at Southeast Missouri State University. She has contributed to teacher education efforts in Missouri for 24 years. Her research interests include early childhood teachers' characteristics, attitudes, and behaviors, and international teaching.

Rosemary Geiken is an associate professor at East Tennessee State University in the early childhood program. She worked with Regents' Center in developing the Ramps and Pathways curriculum as well as other physical knowledge curricula for early childhood.

Deanna Gilkerson lives in Brookings, South Dakota. She is a professor of early childhood education at South Dakota State University.

Alyse C. Hachey, PhD, is an associate professor in the Teacher Education Department at the Borough of Manhattan Community College, City University of New York. She is an educational psychologist whose teaching and research interests focus on early childhood cognition and curriculum development.

Ellen Hall lives in Denver, Colorado, and works at Boulder Journey School. She is the school's founder and executive director. Ellen travels internationally, sharing the work of Boulder Journey School with educators, policy makers, and child advocates. She

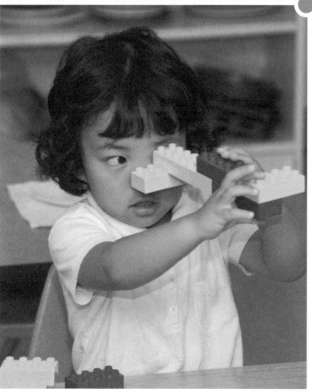

serves on a number of boards and advisory committees, including Videatives, Dimensions Educational Research Foundation, and World Forum Foundation.

Desarie Kennedy, MA, lives in Broomfield, Colorado, and works at Boulder Journey School as a mentor teacher. She is currently a toddler teacher and has taught infants through pre-kindergarten students. She also works for Videatives with Ellen Hall.

Derry Koralek, NAEYC's chief publishing officer, oversees the development of the association's award-winning, research-based periodicals and books. She has worked at NAEYC for nearly 14 years and is the founding editor in chief of *Teaching Young Children*.

Alison Maher works at Boulder Journey School as the education director. She also coordinates a Teacher Certification and Master's Degree program in educational psychology. Over the past two decades, she has worked as a presenter and educational consultant in a wide variety of public and private preschool and elementary schools in the United States, Canada, Australia, and Ireland.

Sarah Normandie is an award-winning law student at Western New England School of Law where she is a merit scholarship recipient. She is a former early childhood educator and Head Start director with more than 12 years of experience teaching young children. Additionally, Sarah is a frequent blogger at 5MinutesforMom.com where she shares ideas to help families and early childhood professionals across the world engage young children in learning through play.

Sue Parrott, MS, is a child development specialist for an Early Head Start and Head Start Program. She was a preschool laboratory instructor at SDSU where she completed research on family and classroom literacy practices.

William C. (Bill) Ritz, professor emeritus of science education at California State University at Long Beach, lives in Southern California. Bill served as Chair of CSULB's Department of Science Education and was director of the Department's "A Head Start on Science" project prior to his retirement.

Julie Sarama, PhD, lives in Denver, Colorado. She works at the University of Denver as a professor and the Kennedy Endowed Chair in Innovative Learning Technologies and Professor.

Elizabeth A. Sherwood, EdD, lives in Glen Carbon, Illinois, and is an associate professor of early childhood education in the Department of Curriculum and Instruction at Southern Illinois University Edwardsville.

Lisa Stevens lives in Denver, Colorado. She is a parent, educator, and former scientist. She completed the Boulder Journey School Teacher Education Program in 2010. Her research and work with children at Boulder Journey School fueled a continued passion for transforming community spaces into creative places for children's authentic learning.

Karyn W. Tunks is professor of elementary and early childhood education at the University of South Alabama in Mobile, Alabama.

Jeanne White, EdD, lives in Tinley Park, Illinois. She is an associate professor and chairperson of the Department of Education at Elmhurst College. There she teaches math methods courses in early childhood, elementary and special education licensure programs. She presents locally and nationally on the topic of mathematics in the early grades and

recently wrote a book for teachers, *Using Children's Literature to Teach Problem Solving in Math: Addressing the Common Core in K-2* (2014, by Taylor and Francis).

Betty Zan, PhD, is associate professor of curriculum and instruction and director of the Regents Center for Early Developmental Education and the Center for Early Education in Science, Technology, Engineering, and Mathematics at the University of Northern Iowa, in Cedar Falls.

TYC
TEACHING YOUNG CHILDREN/PRESCHOOL

Much of the content in this book is adapted from *Teaching Young Children* (*TYC*), NAEYC's award-winning magazine, which celebrates and supports everyone who works with pre-schoolers. Each issue presents practical information through text, photographs, infographics, and illustrations. Short, research-based articles share ideas to use right away.

TYC is available as a member benefit or through subscription. If you like this book, go to www.naeyc.org to join NAEYC or become a *TYC* subscriber.